EVALUATING HUMAN RESOURCES, PROGRAMS, AND ORGANIZATIONS

The Professional Practices in Adult Education and Human Resource Development Series explores issues and concerns of practitioners who work in the broad range of settings in adult and continuing education and human resource development.

The books are intended to provide information and strategies on how to make practice more effective for professionals and those they serve. They are written from a practical viewpoint and provide a forum for instructors, administrators, policy makers, counselors, trainers, managers, program and organizational developers, instructional designers, and other related professionals.

Editorial correspondence should be sent to the Editor-in-Chief:

Michael W. Galbraith
Florida Atlantic University
Department of Educational Leadership
College of Education
Boca Raton, FL 33431

EVALUATING HUMAN RESOURCES, PROGRAMS, AND ORGANIZATIONS

by Byron R. Burnham
Utah State University

KRIEGER PUBLISHING COMPANY
MALABAR, FLORIDA
1995

Original Edition 1995

Printed and Published by
KRIEGER PUBLISHING COMPANY
KRIEGER DRIVE
MALABAR, FLORIDA 32950

Copyright © 1995 by Byron R. Burnham

FROM A DECLARATION OF PRINCIPLES JOINTLY ADOPTED BY A COMMITTEE OF THE AMERICAN BAR ASSOCIATION AND A COMMITTEE OF PUBLISHERS:

This publication is designed to provide accurate and authoritative information in regard to the subject matter covered. It is sold with the understanding that the publisher is not engaged in rendering legal, accounting, or other professional service. If legal advice or other expert assistance is required, the services of a competent professional person should be sought.

Library of Congress Cataloging-In-Publication Data

Burnham, Byron Robert.
    Evaluating human resources, programs and organizations / by Byron
R. Burnham. — Original ed.
        p.   cm. — (Professional practices in adult education and
human resource development series)
    Includes bibliographical references.
    ISBN 0-89464-680-X
    1. Employees—Rating of.   2. Organizational effectiveness—
Evaluation. I. Title. II. Series.
HF5549.5.R3B87   1995
658.4'03—dc20   93-41655
                                                                CIP

10 9 8 7 6 5 4 3 2

CONTENTS

PREFACE

This book is intended for the practitioner of evaluation or for the student who is about to do his or her first formal evaluation. It makes a nice companion volume to other comprehensive texts that supply detailed evaluation approaches and models. The reader will find within these pages reflections about evaluation practice and suggested alternatives to those common everyday problems encountered in doing evaluations.

In this book I share some ideas, problems, considerations, and frustrations I have encountered in doing real life evaluations. Ideas are important because when an evaluator encounters a problem, it is not likely to be solved by going to a cookbook approach. Some people select an evaluation model and then slavishly stick to it. Others (the good ones) use a model as a pattern, and when problems are encountered they think about ways to overcome the problem that may nor may not follow the selected model's pattern.

Problems are not negative occurrences or deviations from plans as the popular dictionary definition indicates. The term *problem* encompasses opportunities, challenges, and situations and is meant to reflect a situation that is amenable to change or solution. Problems often will open the way for people to think in new ways about old situations. Problems are friends waiting to be met. If an evaluator encounters a problem and becomes frustrated and perhaps gives up, he or she will undoubtedly miss opportunities at which others will succeed.

Considerations are those reflections that come to us when we quietly or otherwise look for insight. They come as we think and speculate. Some of the considerations an evaluator should always make are "What if the evaluation comes out this way or that way? What are the alternatives?" Consideration is an in-dispensable part of evaluating.

Frustrations are opportunities to build skills and ask ques-tions. For me, frustrations come when I haven't fully considered the evaluation and all of its ramifications. Frustrations occur in the political area of evaluations. As an evaluator, I cannot let these frustrations overcome my judgments or considerations about the object of study.

I hope that by sharing my ideas, problems, considerations, and frustrations, you are able to examine your evaluation prac-tice and theories. I know that articulating and writing my con-cerns and ideas have affected my practice.

Practitioners will find ideas or viewpoints that may rein-force their ideas or stretch them in considering some alternative points of view. For example, I am not entirely convinced of the common value held among evaluators that external evaluations are more desirable than internal evalautions. One of the prob-lems of being an evaluator is that I am often asked to evaluate programs one day, people the next, and entire organizations or organizational units the next. This book contains a discussion of all three of these aspects within one volume. The reader should look for commonalities among these different tasks. Teachers of evaluation may want to discuss some suggestions I have made with their students. Instuctors may wish to debate my viewpoints with their students. Such a debate will improve understanding of evaluation and ultimately improve its practice.

Chapter 1 offers a map of evaluation. It sets the role of evaluating within the context of an organization and shows how it may be used by the leaders within an organizational con-text. It also discusses one of the critical roles of evaluation: changing people, programs, and organizations.

Chapter 2 discusses personnel appraisals from an evalua-tion standpoint as opposed to a management viewpoint. It pro-vides a brief overview of the development of the personnel appraisal and proposes a systematic approach to this difficult activity.

Chapter 3 uses the perspective of Chapter 2 and offers spe-cific helps in how to set standards, record evidence, analyze data, and make recommendations. The pattern found in Chapter 3 is repeated in Chapters 5 and 7.

Chapter 4 deals with specific examples of each area named in the chapter title by exploring three models of program evaluation: the context, input, process, and product model (CIPP); the naturalistic model; and the connoisseurship model. The chapter also deals with product evaluation as well as evaluating program planning and human resource development outcomes. Addtionally, a framework for judging training programs is provided. Chapter 5 offers a pattern for collection, analysis, and judgment making in these areas.

Chapter 6 explores the evaluation of organizations in areas such as morale, structure, administration, functions, and strategic planning. Chapter 7 follows with a pattern for exploring these areas. Chapter 8 offers some concluding and general thoughts about evaluating.

I hope this book is helpful to field evaluators and that it gives readers a chance to think about their evaluation practice. I appreciate the advice, counsel, and criticism the series editor, Michael Galbraith, has given.

THE AUTHOR

Byron R. Burnham is associate professor of instructional technology and associate dean for learning resources at Utah State University in Logan, Utah. He also serves as evaluation specialist for Utah State University Extension Service. He is senior associate with the Western Institute for Evaluation and Research and has been involved in numerous regional and national evaluation projects. He received his B.S. (1969) and M.S. (1971) degrees from Utah State University in political science. In 1984 he received his doctorate in adult education from the University of British Columbia.

Burnham's major reseach activities have been in the fields of electronic distance education and program planning. His areas of practice include staff development and evaluation. He is book review editor and serves on the editorial advisory board of *Evaluation Practice*. His publications include "Is diversity an inherent part of good evaluation" (1990), "Evaluating the potential effectiveness of electronic distance education systems" (1990), and "Adult learner motivation in electronic distance education" (1991).

Burnham teaches graduate classes in educational research and philosophy. He received the 1990–91 Charles Wedemyer Award from the *American Journal of Distance Education* and the University of Wisconsin. He is currently an intern in the National Extension Leadership Development Program.

CHAPTER 1

Evaluation: An Introduction

This chapter introduces evaluation and places it in a context that will be familiar to managers, educators, and trainers. It sets the framework for the following chapters by considering the relationship of evaluation to leadership. The activities of finding truth, making judgments, and changing people are considered. While these aspects of evaluation are lofty and are not often talked about, they are important to people involved in evaluation because they affect an evaluator's actions. When a person has considered his or her philosophical basis for action, those actions will be consistent and rational.

In the last part of this chapter, the role of reporting and using the results of reports are considered. This seems like a hugh jump from lofty consideration of philosophy to mundane reporting; however, philosophy and reporting are related because our beliefs about "what is" should affect our actions (that is, reporting and using evaluations). The organization of Chapter 1 follows the purposes and procedures of evaluation.

Before evaluation is considered as an act of leading, certain terms need to be defined. Within these pages, the term *adult educator* is used in the broadest sense possible. Not many people who educate adults think of themselves as adult educators. For example, corporate trainers who are involved in management development would not consider themselves adult educators even though they are very much involved in educating adults. I see adult educators wherever I go, in a variety of settings. In a sense, I see managers being involved in adult education activities from time to time. It should be obvious that adult education is not limited to a schooling setting.

From time to time the term *adult education unit* is used. This refers to a continuing education division in a college or university, a training division in a company or corporation, or an adult education division in a library. Again, the implication from this definition is that adult education is a broad endeavor.

Corporations and *companies* are terms used to help those in the private sector feel somewhat comfortable with the book and at the same time expand the vision of those of us in education. From the standpoint of evaluation, there is little wrong with thinking about educational organizations as corporations or companies. Public and private organizations have a lot in common.

The term *evaluator* refers to anyone who perform evaluative tasks. On one occasion it may mean a trained evaluator, while it may refer to a manager or supervisor who briefly engages in evaluation activities on another occasion. Again, this term is used broadly.

This interchange of terms should help the reader as evaluation is explored. The broadest use of these terms will aid in understanding evaluator activity.

LEADERSHIP AND EVALUATION

Sometimes evaluators get caught in the leadership trap of believing that they, as an evaluator, are not part of the management team. Whether a person is acting as an external or an internal evaluator, the trap is an easy one in which to get caught. I have experienced the trap a number of times and it is a disconcerting feeling. My full-time employment is by a university wherein I do evaluations for the unit for which I work. I have served as an outside evaluator a number of times in a number of different contexts, and the trap is the same no matter what my role is. People view an evaluator as an extension of the management team. I have tried with limited success to have people view me as something other than management.

What is the harm in being viewed as part of management? The problem is the quality of the information an evaluator gets.

All evaluators want their work to be valid. If an evaluator is viewed as management, then information given tends to be what people think management wants to hear, thus decreasing its validity.

An internal evaluator, if he or she is effective, will continually work with management in order to get evaluation results acted upon, again enlarging the trap. An external evaluator is usually hired by management to find something about opinions or impacts. The evaluator works closely with management in focusing the evaluation, again enlarging the trap.

While the trap is always there, some things can be done to minimize the problem. One of them is just being aware of it. This awareness helps evaluators understand one of the limitations facing valid studies.

More active steps include:

1. Allowing others who have a stake in the evaluation to guide the design and use of evaluation results. Examples of these persons include managers, funders, workers, clients, and participants.

2. Reporting the results to all stakeholders, not just management. Sometimes information is collected on a private basis and cannot be shared widely because of the sensitive nature of the evaluation or contractual obligations. A good evaluator will know when those situations pertain, and more often than not most information can and should be widely shared.

3. Structuring the evaluation so it includes an action component aimed at use of the findings. This component should include representatives from beyond the management group. A weakness common to both internal and external evaluation is that results may not be used. Use is different from merely accepting the evaluation results. Assume for a moment that you have completed an evaluation and the results have been accepted by management but are not acted upon. Such an evaluation benefits no one. Results have to be used to be valuable. If an evaluator can build into a project an

action committee that becomes active after results have been published and the evaluator withdraws, then the objectivity of the evaluator is preserved and the organization benefits from the study. This meets the objection of the evaluator becoming a consultant in correcting the problem.

4. Defining the evaluator's status as nonmanagement whenever possible. This is a danger in terms of losing influence with the decisions makers. However, a balance must be maintained between influencing management and having access to unbiased data. Let me give an example. I am a staff evaluator; my office is next door to the associate vice president and he and I share the same secretary. I meet on a regular basis with a group of managers and frequently with the vice president's staff. The rest of the organization knows this and I am perceived as "administration" by most of them. For a number of years I fought (with little success) this perception. Then I began to realize that such a perception could be an asset in terms of getting evaluation results used and in getting delicate and sensitive evaluations approved.

The balance comes in keeping the evaluation information valid. This is done by building trust through keeping confidences with my colleagues. I do not participate in decision making, even though I strive to influence those decisions. I have spoken openly about my role with the vice president and his associate. They understand and are quite willing to let me function this way.

But what about my colleagues? This is a different matter to be sure. I explain my role to them on a one-on-one basis and involve them in constructing evaluations. If they request an evaluation or if they ask my help in doing one, then they "own" the information and they control its use. Again, the administration respects this way of operating and have never asked me to supply information from an evaluation they did not sponsor. My nonmanagement colleagues know this and understand the information is theirs to use however they wish.

I have designed a personnel appraisal system to be used by

management in appraising my colleagues and myself. Field staff know this, but they also know that I do not do appraisals, and that I am open to their suggestions about how a personnel appraisal system should be designed. This trust is based on several years of working together and building trust.

This fine line of valid and useable information is one that can either haunt an evaluator or be a tool in accomplishing the work. The evaluator has the most influence on how he or she is viewed.

FORMATIVE AND SUMMATIVE EVALUATION

The trap discussed above does not change whether the evaluation is formative or summative. Many authors have made distinctions between these two forms of evaluation. The distinctions are noted in the roots of the two words. *Formative* evaluation is used to guide the implementation and management of an evaluation. It *forms* or in*forms* the program by acting like the internal guidance system of a rocket providing corrective information as it moves toward a target.

*Sum*mative evaluation is often conducted at the end of program and is used to make some judgment about how well the program did and how worthwhile it was. It *sums* the program results. It provides a total worth of an evaluation object and is used for accountability purposes.

Most authors acknowledge these two differences and then move on to talk about evaluation as though there are no differences. Formative evaluation is easier to do and is usually welcomed by stakeholders. Summative is more difficult, is less welcomed by some stakeholders, and in some cases is even openly resisted.

Formative evaluation requires different kinds of evidence from summative evaluation (these different kinds of evidence will be discussed more fully in chapter 2). Whether one is engaged in summative or formative evaluation, he or she is engaged in a search for truth.

LOOKING FOR TRUTH

Most evaluation activities are not aimed at collecting evidence, but rather at finding truth. Collecting evidence is one way to establish truth. Many, if not all, philosophers have considered the nature of truth with differing results. It is not our job nor is there enough space in this book to consider the issue of truth, so I offer a definition I think most evaluators use. Truth in terms of evaluation lies in those circumstances that most closely conform to reality. This further defines reality as being objective and at times measurable.

Therefore, the fundamental job of evaluation is to describe reality, but such a description is not very useful to a frontline evaluator. What is useful is the notion that evaluators' efforts are attempts at providing evidence that certain conditions pertain and that they have evidence demonstrating causation of the events to some degree. This is done through data collection, analysis, reporting, and heavy doses of logic.

Lately, there has been discussion about the ages of evaluation. Guba and Lincoln (1989) write about the four generations of evaluation: Generation One was a technical age where in evaluators measured things; Generation Two was a time when evaluators described things; Generation Three was a judgmental age wherein evaluators made judgments about the worth or merit of programs or people; and Generation Four is a negotiation age wherein evaluators help various stakeholders come to some agreement about what "is." These ages may appear to be a clean and tidy way of describing the history of looking for truth. Reflecting on what Lincoln and Guba have written, I conclude that these are not ages of evaluation. Instead, they seem to be roles for an evaluator at various points within an evaluation project.

In various evaluations, I have played each of those roles, and I have not found any sequence to those roles. At times I can measure things. At other times I have to judge. But most often, it seems the role of negotiator is played because people are often unclear about what they want from an evaluation and even what objectives they have in mind for a program or an organization.

For example, one evaluation in which I was recently involved included several directors of educational programs who could not agree on the overall purpose of a program that was to be evaluated. We began looking at what should be evaluated and built a list of questions to be answered. They could not agree, not only on the questions but on the very level of questioning. They needed negotiation in order to begin the evaluation. Negotiation means more than bargaining for a widely held view of reality. It also means bargaining for approaches to studying reality.

MAKING JUDGMENTS

One thing that makes evaluations different from research is judgment making. We collect all kinds of data just as researchers do and often under similar kinds of conditions. We are concerned about issues of validity and reliability just as researchers are. These issues lead us to look much like researchers. In fact, at my university there is a graduate program titled the "Research and Evaluation Methodology Program." Somewhere someone recognized these two endeavors are very closely allied.

In spite of similarities, there are things that make evaluators different from researchers. One is the notion of judging, which moves evaluation from science into art. Most scientists do not make judgments because doing so involves values that according to the canons of science cannot be allowed. Scientists use words like *functional* and *dysfunctional*. Evaluators have to be comfortable with words like *good* and *bad*.

Thus, judgment making gives evaluators a distinction and a burden. How do they go about making those kinds of judgments? How do they prove their conclusions? That's what evaluation is about.

CHANGE

Change is one of the most fundamental aspects of life. As Roman philosopher Marcus Aurelius noted, "Everything is in a state of change. Thou, thyself art in everlasting change and in corruption to correspond, so is the whole universe" (Infobases International, 1992). Change is acknowledged by all as being a constant, but some, like Karl Marx, have seen it as an outcome to be sought for. Marx wrote, "The philosophers have only interpreted the world; the thing, however is to change it" (Infobases International, 1992).

This is an expected outcome from evaluation. One of the basic assumptions of evaluation is that it is done in order to change something or someone. And sometimes in order to change something, people must be changed.

Changing People

Personnel appraisals are often conducted with the idea that they are a type of evaluation and that the outcome of such endeavors ought to be change. While this may be true to a point, a number of things need to be considered first. People make fundamental changes because they want to and not because someone else wants them to. Many employees patiently wait for performance appraisals to be finished so they can get back to what they are doing, with little thought of making changes.

It is a given that people will change if they have the needed information to make a change, if the information is nonthreatening, and if it is presented in a nonthreatening manner.

One of the fundamental understandings that Knowles (1980) has provided the field of adult education practice is the notion that humans are who they are because of experiences. If humans learn things that conflict with their "core person," they will reject that learning and not change. The implications for those who are in the business of changing people is obvious: Methods can not be used to make threats and data must be presented for consideration, not inclusion, in a person's life. After all, each human has his or her agency and can accept or reject that information.

Finally, an evaluator must acknowledge that he can only change his own behavior and not the behavior of someone else. Therefore, a supervisor who is charged with personnel appraisal, and by logical deduction personal change, must recognize that her task is limited to herself.

Changing Organizations

Organization change is a difficult topic that requires several perspectives. It is my intention to link organization change with people change, but I realize it is broader and more complex than just that. In fact, organizations are comprised of people, structures, and processes. If you want to change an organization, then you can attempt to change either the people, the structure, or the processes. The reason I will link the change of people and organizations is because this linkage is often intellectually made, but is rarely made in practice. We will explore some practical ways to link the two. I am thinking here of the organization that purposefully builds a culture, a way of doing things in the organization.

Changing Programs

There is a large field of practice termed *program evaluation*. It is not only large but also complex. The outcome of program evaluation is often change. It also involves accountability or the notion of how well a program has done what it intended to do.

How does one know when a program change is needed? What are the standards used to judge a program? Can these standards be transferred from one program to another, or are they all program specific? That is to say are they tied to a program's unique objectives or are there standards that are some how transferrable from program to program? If not, then how can one judge (and hence choose) between two programs that both require scarce resources?

These questions with implementation guides are discussed in chapter 4. For now, lets just keep the questions in mind.

POLITICS IN EVALUATION

All evaluations are political. Whenever I hear that statement I recall my first evaluation. I can't remember who it was for or what it was for, but I do remember it was not a very controversial one. It was straightforward, it was simple, and it was political. Being a new evaluator, I didn't realize that people have much invested in their professional turf and that political concerns can come from a variety of sources.

The nature of politics needs to be defined here. This does not refer to the Republican, Democrat, NDP, Conservative, or Liberal type of politics. Rather, the political science concept of politics that concerns itself with the notion of power and influence is used here. Evaluators should be in tune with this concept. Evaluators have power and influence, and power and influence will be exerted on them. Evaluators are the finders of answers, (and so people will try to give them the answers) and the makers of judgments (and so people will try to give them the judgments).

Does this sound like a big and weighty job? It is. When an evaluator has this in mind, he or she may act with needed caution and a desire to "get it right."

It is usually perceived that evaluations will have winners and losers. This perception adds to the political nature of evaluation activities. One way to overcome the political nature is to recognize and empower the numerous stakeholders in an evaluation activity. Empowerment is not the hollow word as many people use it today. Instead, it reflects an operating philosophy for the evaluator.

Steps to empowerment in evaluation are:

1. Encourage the people who will be affected to make the decisions about what will be evaluated and how it will be evaluated. This does not mean encouraging people to use less than rigorous methods. It does mean encouraging them to influence the evaluator's thinking about the means and ends of evaluation.

2. Help management to see stakeholder opinion as a valid and considered position. (This brings into evaluation activities the negotiation aspect Guba and Lincoln (1989) have discussed.)

3. Structure the evaluation activity to include an advisory committee of stakeholders. This will be expanded beyond the normal evaluation management group and may include opponents of the evaluation and even critics of the methods or objectives of the evaluation.

4. Report the results of the evaluation so that action is expected from the stakeholders. This can be an action planning session wherein stakeholders plan the next steps once they have the evaluation results. Of course, for any such plan to be successful, the decision makers need to be involved not only in the planning session but in the very act of planning the planning session.

While empowerment of stakeholders sounds (and is) lofty, it can be accomplished in rather mundane ways. One of the most mundane and often least used ways is reporting. Reporting is essential for evaluators and they must dutifully report evaluation results; however, few use them for empowerment. The following sections show how useful reports can be constructed that allow change to take place.

MAKING EVALUATION REPORTS

The section above assumes that an evaluation report will be made. It is surprising to know that not many evaluators plan to make a report. They assume one will be written and delivered to the people who have asked for the evaluation, but they do not plan how this will be done. Such a plan needs to be thought about early in the process.

Evaluation reports can be divided into traditional and nontraditional categories. Traditional reports are usually written and given to the people who ask for the evaluation to be conducted. The following suggestions will make the report more widely read and perhaps used.

Traditional written reports should be in at least three sections. The first and shortest part of the report should be aimed at people who have little time or interest in reading a detailed report. This executive summary should be no longer than one or two pages and should be written in point form. Major conclusions and recommendations should be presented in short statements that can be skimmed quickly. The summary should be written with the idea that people who read the report may or may not be familiar with the subject of study or its methods. It is useful to imagine that the person or persons who asked you to do the report will want to show it to his or her boss. (This has implications for the person the evaluator talks with before the evaluation begins in order to find out what his or her boss would like to see in an evaluation.)

The second part of the report should contain the detailed findings and recommendations, the evidence for those findings and recommendations, and the methods used in locating the evidence and coming to the conclusions. This section will be of interest to those who asked for the evaluation to be done and for those who want to understand how it was done.

The third part of the report should contain the data that contributed to the findings and recommendations. I have included in this section the frequencies from surveys, statistical tests and results, and transcripts from interviews where appropriate (sometimes it is not appropriate because of promises of anonymity). These can be labeled as appendices and sometimes are comprised of computer printouts in tabular form.

Traditional report making is the backbone of the evaluation project. It is a means to reach the final goal of evaluations: to make a difference.

Nontraditional report making includes videotaped reports, open forums, debates, and other such means. Making reports via videotapes is a skill that evaluators should gain, or they should employ someone from the field of video production. If a videotape contains a talking head, then it is really nothing more than a variation of the traditional written report. By a videotape report I mean something that is hard hitting, short, and to the point and that uses the medium to it fullest advantage.

For example, imagine Barbara Walters providing the report. She would use a mix of narrative, interviews, actual video footage of events, some differing opinions, debates, and a conclusion. All of these segments would be edited to provide easy and interesting watching. If all a videotaped report includes is one narrator and some charts, then such material should be put in a written report that allows readers to flip through the pages quickly and at their discretion rather than having to follow the linear nature of a videotape.

Meetings that present the findings in a speech are traditional report forms; however, those meetings which allow some comment and perhaps even spirited discussion can be classified as nontraditional. The nontraditional form requires action before the meeting to insure that people will have read the report and are willing to enter into discussion, or at least that varying points of view are represented.

USING EVALUATION RESULTS

Evaluations are nothing more than a study of a program unless the results are used. Use of information changes a study into an evaluation. It seems logical then that an evaluator should spend time thinking about and planning for the use of the information obtained from an evaluation.

Use should drive the kinds of questions asked in an evaluation, the kinds of stakeholders involved in an evaluation, and the kinds of reports made about the evaluation. Whenever I begin an evaluation, I ask the person who initially contacts me,

"What do you want to know and why do you want to know it?" Additional questions include, "What do you intend to do because of the evaluation?" All three of these questions have to do with use of the results. Answers to these questions help define the stakeholders who should be involved in the evaluation.

If the evaluation is intended to change a program in some way (and I maintain that both summative and formative evaluation have program change as either an expressed or an assumed outcome), then the following stakeholders should be involved: program managers, program staff, funders, and program clients. If the evaluation is a personnel evaluation or a performance appraisal, then the stakeholders include supervisors, employees, and management. It is evident that the stakeholder with the most at stake is the employee, so the employee is the stakeholder who should have the highest degree of involvement. However, merely identifying and involving appropriate stakeholders is not enough.

Once stakeholders are identified, they can then make plans for the use of the evaluation. A meeting for the express purpose of planning for the use of the results should be held with the stakeholders. It is true that the results of the evaluation will to a degree help determine what course of action should be taken; however, plans for implementation can be made at a macro level. For example, if a program that taught people how to be better financial managers was being evaluated, then certain steps can be outlined before the evaluation ever begins. These steps include reporting the results to appropriate people and deciding how to make changes, how to implement changes, how to monitor the changes, and how to provide reports to other interested people. These simple steps are not detailed and can be changed and modified rather easily. Importantly, the expectation that the results will be used has been established.

Even more important than establishing the expectation is the way in which the evaluation is carried out. The following scenarios point out an evaluation that will likely be used and one that probably will not be used. Evaluation Project A involves decision makers at all critical points. It "feeds forward" important and tentative findings before the project is completed. It asks for critique of the evaluation as it is in progress. The contractor for the evaluation is involved in appropriate ways in the management of the evaluation.

Evaluation Project B offers little or no opportunity for stakeholder involvement except as a source of information for the study. It makes an interim report and a final report. The contractor does not see evaluation results except at the interim report and the final report. Which of these projects is likely to result in a "used" evaluation? The greatest complement that can be paid to an evaluator is for his or her study to be used in some way. Otherwise, it is nothing.

SUMMARY

This chapter provided an overview of evaluation in terms of philosophy and linked philosophical considerations to important evaluation tasks like reporting. It began by discussing a leadership trap that often ensnares evaluators and then pointed out how leadership and evaluation are related. Change was discussed from the perspective of people, organizations, and programs. Some time was spent in reviewing reports and their use in effecting change. One message of the chapter is that philosophy and action are rather directly linked. The following chapters provide a more contextualized look at evaluation activities and how context may effect the way we evaluate.

CHAPTER 2

Evaluating People

Designing and conducting performance appraisals is perhaps the most difficult task facing evaluators and human resource development (HRD) administrators and managers. This task is intensified when it occurs in a unit where the work is different from the rest of the organization. For example, in adult education units the nature of the work differs from other parts of organizations. After all, in which other parts of an organization does an individual engage in needs assessment, program planning, instruction, counseling, budgeting, marketing, social action, and evaluating? Because adult educators and HRD administrators are often involved in evaluating, we may tend to confuse program evaluation with performance appraisal. This chapter demonstrates how program evaluation is related to, but different from, performance appraisal. It describes a performance appraisal system that has enough flexibility that it can be used in the many contexts in which adult educators, human resource developers, and others work. After reading this chapter an evaluator should be able to consider elements like standards and processes as he or she develops a performance appraisal system.

DIFFERENCES BETWEEN PERFORMANCE APPRAISAL AND PROGRAM EVALUATION

Sometimes we evaluate a product or program a person has created and confuse that activity with evaluating the person. Program evaluation is broader than performance appraisal and usually does not use quality of staff efforts as the only gauge of program success. The quality of program inputs (staff efforts) are sometimes evaluated as part of a larger examination of program success. However, the end of program evaluation is seldom an assessment of staff performance. Program evaluation can help in performance evaluation. To understand how this can be done, the nature of performance appraisal needs to be explored.

THE THREE "AGES" OF
PERFORMANCE APPRAISAL

There have been at least three distinct ages of performance appraisal. The first and most crude we can call "character appraisal," where personality plays a large part in assessing various characteristics of staff members. Questions like "Is he or she easy to get along with?" are asked. This kind of performance appraisal is often subjective, is biased, uses irrelevant items, and helps establish "good old" persons' networks.

The second age of performance appraisal is a bit more sophisticated and seems to be prevalent in today's business settings. It is behaviorally based and criterion-referenced. In other words, it is based on judging behaviors by criteria taken from job descriptions used to advertise positions and to screen applicants. The criteria are job-specific. Questions such as "Does the individual submit reports in a timely manner?" are asked. One advantage of this kind of performance appraisal is that it is more objective and the assessor can make clearer judgments than in the first kind of performance appraisal.

The newest age of performance appraisal is based on how well established objectives have been met. The objectives are mutually established by supervisors and employees. They are stated in terms of program achievements, personal development, program planning skills, or other such matters. Questions such as "How well has the objective established during the last performance appraisal session been met?" are asked. It is the nature of the objective that sets the parameters of the performance appraisal. One advantage is objectivity in performance appraisals. This objectivity is enhanced when set objectives are stated in clearly measurable terms. For example, one objective may be to increase the number of programs developed in one year from 3 to 20. There can be little bias in appraising an employee's performance against such a goal. Another advantage is that staff members can be involved in establishing these goals and, as a result, share ownership in the performance appraisal system. In other words, performance appraisal then becomes something employees do for themselves rather than something that is done to them.

There are disadvantages to objective-based performance appraisal. One is the fact that goals may not be achieved because of factors beyond the control of the employee. For this reason it may not be fair to judge personnel on the basis of program success or failure. The task is to identify those factors that lie within the control of staff members as the basis for the professional's objectives and appraisal.

A PROPOSED SYSTEM

The system proposed here is a systematic approach to performance appraisal and is highly adaptive to the many different organizational roles. Elman and Smock (1985) proposed a matrix approach to performance appraisal that considers the kind of work performed, the evidence for that work, the assessors, the criteria, and the weighing of the criteria. Their framework was developed for a higher education setting; however, it is easily adapted to many different organizations. They used teaching, scholarship, grants and contracts, and service as work categories in addressing higher education performance appraisals. This approach is used in Table 2.1, which outlines how an adult educator's or corporate trainer's work in higher education and business might be assessed. (Throughout this chapter I will use an adult educator as an example of how this system can be em-

Table 2.1 A schema for assessing adult education performance

Work categories	Sources of evidence	Reviewers	Criteria	Weighting
Originating program ideas	Written program descriptions, program listings, letters	Other adult educators, supervisors	Number, relevance, utility	Low to high
Developing program ideas	Committee work, program listings, comments from colleagues	Other adult educators, supervisors	Number, quality, completeness, relevance	Low to high
Establishing program objectives	Written objectives	Supervisors, collaborating faculty	Relevance, level of change (knowledge, practice, etc.), utility	Medium to high
Selecting and sequencing learning activities	Program structure as indicated from published information	Colleagues	Relevance to objectives, level of change, learner participation	Medium to high
Insuring participation (advertising, PR, cooperation, etc.)	Advertising campaign, letters of agreement, etc.	Supervisors	Number of attendees, number of cooperators	High
Securing Resources	Financial statements, reports	Supervisors	Program costs and benefits	High
Evaluating	Instruments, data, reports	Colleagues, supervisors	Level of Bennett's hierarchy	High

ployed.) The work categories come from program planning tasks common to many adult educators.

Use of the Proposed System

Because the matrix approach can accommodate two factors, it is a flexible system that can be designed to fit the many circumstances. While the reward process (sources of evidence, reviewers, criteria, and weighting) may be similar from situation to situation, the work categories are not necessarily as constant. For example, some adult educators are involved in teaching and do not plan programs. For these individuals, work categories should reflect instructional tasks such as preparing lesson outlines, developing instructional objectives, and student performance. The flexibility in changing work categories allows the system to fit the context for any adult educator.

The kind of objectives established determine if a performance appraisal will be primarily quantitative or qualitative in nature. For example, an adult educator and supervisor may mutually agree that during the coming year it is very important to develop 10 more program ideas than during the past year. This agreement would define the goals for that work category in a quantitative manner. If, however, a decision was made for the adult educator to develop one program idea that had implications for the state or province and the nation, then the definition of the goal would be mainly qualitative in nature. The proposed system accommodates either approach.

PROGRAM EVALUATION
AND PERFORMANCE APPRAISAL

Program evaluation is based on the assessment of program outcomes and can be a source both of evidence and processes for performance appraisal. Bennett (1976) has described a hierarchy of program evaluation evidence that he maintains becomes more important as the levels of evidence are ascended.

7. End results
6. Practice change
5. Knowledge, attitudes, skills, and aspirations (KASA) change
4. Reactions
3. People involvement
2. Activities
1. Inputs

Figure 2.1   Bennett's hierarchy of program evidence

Evidence for performance appraisal can be selected from the hierarchy. As a part of the performance appraisal activity, the hierarchy is useful in helping employees set goals. For example, certain staff members may have primary responsibility for activities at Level 5 and others at Level 3. The important factor is that in objective-based performance appraisal staff members are assessed at mutually agreed upon levels. Figure 2.1 displays Bennett's hierarchy.

This hierarchy results from analyzing the chain of events that occurs in all adult education programs. "Inputs" or resources are used to produce "activities" for people who have "reactions." Because of their involvement, people gain "knowledge, attitudes, skills, or aspirations" that lead to "practice changes" that, in turn, have "end results." Bennett reformatted these events into levels of evidence and, in this way, produced his hierarchy.

The first three levels of the hierarchy contain data that are easily obtained. Level 1 represents input data that include time spent in organizing activities, costs incurred, and other resources used. Level 2 represents activity data that include courses, classes, and other events. Level 3 represents people involvement data that include numbers of people, frequency of participation, and participant characteristics. All of these data are easily collected and are readily available for analysis.

Moving through the hierarchy to Level 4 represents a shift from data that are easily obtained to data that require some additional effort to capture. Participants' reactions to programs have long been the traditional approach to evaluating adult education programs, and most evaluations do not move beyond this level. Usually, these first four levels represent evidence that lends itself to formative evaluation. The next three levels of evidence lend themselves to summative evaluation.

Level 5 represents another shift in the nature of evaluative data. These data represent evidence of skill achievement, attitude shifts, and knowledge gains. At this level, evaluation becomes complex with comparative tests implied. Level 6 represents data about changes in lifestyles, use of skills, application of knowledge, and adoption of attitudes. Level 7 represents data about the consequences of changes at the other levels of the hierarchy. Evidence from the top part of the hierarchy is more difficult and more expensive to gather than evidence from the bottom part of the hierarchy; however, top-level evidence can be used to document an adult educator's efforts and assist him or her in performance appraisal.

Evidence from Bennett's hierarchy can be used in supplying evidence for performance appraisal as noted in the "Evaluating" work category from Figure 2.1. These levels in effect become the "Criteria" for the reward process. In effect, the levels at which program evaluation is conducted become the criteria for performance appraisal and the outcome of program evaluation becomes the evidence for performance appraisal.

Weighting of the criteria is dependent on the very culture of the organization to which an adult educator belongs. For example, in one continuing education organization, profit from programs drives the unit, while social concerns are more important in another unit. These two kinds of units would likely weigh the criteria differently.

The framework presented here demonstrates a systematic approach to the difficult task of performance appraisal. It can involve the employee who is being assessed, and it can become a less traumatic task if it is done more often than annually. Performance appraisal can either be a formative or a summative exercise. That is, it can be a developmental exercise or a final review of activities. The more successful approach will be one that provides frequent feedback and opportunities for success.

USING MANAGEMENT OBJECTIVES
IN PERFORMANCE APPRAISAL

Management objectives refer to those objectives set by management for either the organization or the individual. Whichever they refer to, it is assumed that the individual employee has significant input into which objectives are established. The organizational objectives are used to set personnel-related objectives. For example, if an organization has as its goal to provide better service to a certain part of the country, then the negotiated performance appraisal objectives for individual employees should reflect that fact. Such objectives can inform much of what is done in this regard.

INVOLVING THE EMPLOYEE
IN PERFORMANCE APPRAISAL

One of the fundamental mistakes often made by supervisors is not involving employees in the process of personnel appraisal other than as the object of assessment. No wonder it is a difficult and dreaded experience for people. People resent the fact they are judged. A solution is meaningful involvement in the design, conduct, and conclusion of performance appraisals. Just as a cardinal rule exists for the involvement of stakeholders in evaluation, so it should be a cardinal rule for performance appraisals.

Employees can be involved in performance appraisal in a number of different ways. One way is in designing performance appraisal. Rather than pulling a form for performance appraisal from the shelf, the items included in performance appraisal should be considered by the people who are going to be assessed. In organizations it may be impossible for all people to be involved in selecting the items. However, it is possible for representatives to be involved.

Another way of involving people is to ask for comments from employees before a formal performance appraisal system is put in place. The entire plan should be presented for comment or a vote or both. If the comments or the vote are negative, the proposed plan should be revised in light of comments from employees. Such actions are desirable before a system is put in place and employee concerns are made known in other, less desirable ways.

FOLLOWING UP PERFORMANCE APPRAISALS

One common mistake made in appraising employees is that it happens only once a year. Employees are expected to undergo a difficult and emotional experience that will have implications for the coming year in terms of promotion or merit salary increases. More frequent assessment and feedback reduces stress and provides a more accurate reading of a person's performance than do annual sessions.

Stress is reduced because the judgment does not have year-long implications. It is a bit like the Winter Olympics where once every 4 years the bobsled races take place. Participants are very keyed up because they know this is a quadrennial occurrence. Skiing competitors are a bit more relaxed because they know another major competition is only weeks away. If an employee knows that he or she has only 3 months to carry a "less than satisfactory" rating, then he or she can begin to make corrections to be evaluated only weeks away. Another dimension is that employees who are rated "very good" will continue to work to keep that standing current.

Accuracy of the judgment will also increase because of the numerous points of "measure." (See Figure 2.2). The advantage of numerous reporting or observation periods is obvious. In each case, if only one reading was taken the conclusions would be mistaken. More measures and observations make them more accurate.

In each of the cases represented in Figure 2.2, if performance appraisals had occurred at only annual intervals (time 4), the ratings of employees would not tell as complete a story as other review times (times 1-8). However, when multiple measures are considered there are different patterns for each em-

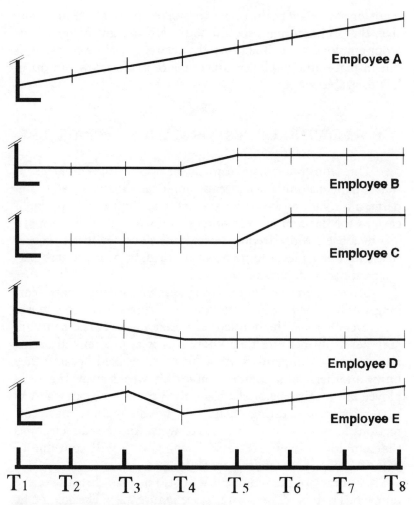

Figure 2.2 Time series observations

ployee. Employee E, while rated at the lowest level, is making as much progress as employee A who was rated at the highest level. Employee D has plateaued and is not making progress. Employee B seems to make progress around annual appraisal time only. Employee C makes some progress after the annual review.

Performance appraisal should be thought of as a continuous process whenever supervisors and employees talk about work. Activities include unscheduled meetings about work and work-related tasks. When meetings include feedback that will let employees know how they are doing, some kind of notation about the meeting should be made by the supervisor such as a follow-up letter regarding the visit and what was talked about.

These kinds of meetings and follow-up or feedback allow both the supervisor and employee to speak about midcourse corrections so that the overall target or goal set during a formalized performance appraisal session will more likely be achieved. To do otherwise would be like launching an Apollo mission to the moon and never giving the astronauts information about how the spacecraft was proceeding or where it was located in terms of its projected course. Supervisors should employ some kind of strategy that will allow employees to know how they are doing in terms of targets and procedures at almost any time during a year or other performance appraisal cycle. This implies frequent and shared performance appraisal activities. We have already discussed what frequent might mean. Shared performance appraisal activities refer to either the supervisor or employee initiating, with the agreement of the other, a performance appraisal feedback session. My feeling is that unless employees ask for feedback, it will not be taken seriously. Feedback, to be effective, must be requested.

PERFORMANCE APPRAISAL AND HIRING

When someone is hired, a role description should be written by the employee with the concurrence and assistance of the supervisor. Problems associated with poor performance are often traced to hiring without a meaningful job description. Job descriptions and consequent role descriptions become a screen for merit increases and promotions. A job description is rooted in performance terms. In other words, employees know what it is they are to do on the job. As will be shown later, various levels of performance can help both the employer and employee understand how well a job is being performed.

The issue of hiring someone who does not meet every requirement of a job description is real. Some requirements are likely to be either missed or exceeded. Agreement on the role by both the supervisor and employee is a necessary step. It is the old issue of involving the employee. There maybe some areas in which a newly hired employee is not at all competent, and at the same time, it is likely there are areas where expectations are exceeded. For these reasons, the employee and supervisor should agree on how the role description can be modified to meet the personal needs of the employee and the group needs of the company or agency.

This kind of accommodation benefits both parties because new talents can be used by the organization and areas of frustration for the employee are eliminated. This is not to say there is radical change from the job description to the role description; rather, it is a way of fine tuning job descriptions so they are largely met by a candidate.

The revised role description forms the foundation for future performance appraisals. It is from the description that standards are then developed for use during performance appraisals.

PERFORMANCE APPRAISAL AND PROMOTING

The success of performance appraisal efforts depends on how performance appraisals results are used. Consider the following two examples. In Organization A, the performance appraisal effort is scheduled throughout the year. At least four formal performance appraisal meetings are held with employees during that time. Additionally, informal performance appraisal takes place. Whenever employees are recognized for excellent performance or cited for poor performance, a letter is sent to them with specific statements about what was done correctly or what was done incorrectly. These letters become part of a performance appraisal portfolio.

In Organization B, performance appraisal is a formal

meeting held yearly. There are adequate forms to complete and the employees know just where they stand at the end of a session. In fact, they sign a form stating they understand what has been presented, and they may or may not agree with the verdict. Soon after the meeting is held, salary increases are announced.

The questions that an evaluator asks about the two systems include: What are the purposes of performance appraisal? Who wants the information? and How will the information be used? The following are answers to these three questions using the two examples.

1. What are the purposes of performance appraisal? In Organization A, the purposes are to provide employees with frequent and useable information so they can make changes. These changes can be made in time for salary increases. In Organization B, the purposes are to decide who will get a salary increase and at what level.

2. Who wants the information? In Organization A, the information is wanted by the employees so they can make changes as needed in order to do a better job and improve personal skills. In Organization B, the supervisors want the information.

3. How will the information be used? In Organization A, the information will be used by employee to do two things. One is to make changes as already noted and the other is to develop their personal record of performance. This personal record can be used at a formal performance appraisal meeting by both the employee and supervisor. They meet on more equal terms than do the supervisors and employees in Organization B where the use of the information is to decide who gets an increase and how large that increase is.

When job promotions come available (either within or outside a organization), the employees with portfolios stand a better chance of gaining a promotion. Organizations should be in the business of building people. This can be accomplished by internal or external promotion. I have interviewed a number of employees to discover what they think about performance appraisal and linking it to salary increases. A typical comment is, "It is the single biggest morale destroyer around here." People want feedback about how they are doing, but they do not want it tied directly to salary increases.

Performance appraisal systems differ. Some are poor and others are excellent. Poor and excellent systems can be differentiated by the following characteristics: feedback, frequent sessions, shared ownership, employee involvement, and specificity in ratings.

Developing Scales for Performance Appraisal

A common concern expressed by employees who are subjected to poor personnel appraisals is that they don't know what "average" or "above average" means. If your system uses these kinds of summative terms without defining them, consider revising it before it is used again. In reality, "average" has no place in assessing the performance of people unless a system involves the computation of means and standard deviations; then such measures should be valid and reliable. Achieving this status requires a systematic study of the rating instrument and is a costly and time-consuming effort.

Some scales are anchored at the all points of the scale, while others are anchored at the two endpoints of a scale as illustrated in Figure 2.3.

The decision about whether one should fully or partly anchor scales is best made on the basis of two factors. One is the purpose. Sometimes behaviors need to be fully described at each step. The other factor is the ability to describe completely the behavior being rated. If words cannot describe the behaviors in between the continuum ends, then only the endpoints should be anchored.

How many points should be put on a scale? Some would argue for 9, others for 7, still others for 5, and yet others for 3. I think 9 is too many and becomes a bit difficult for the rater to

A Fully Anchored Scale			
4.	**3.**	**2.**	**1.**
Consistently meets deadlines	Usually meets deadlines	Seldom meets deadlines	Never meets deadlines
A Partially Anchored Scale			
4.	**3.**	**2.**	**1.**
Consistently meets deadlines			Never meets deadlines

Figure 2.3   Anchored scales

distinguish among. I like 4 or 5 as a general rule. On a few occasions I have used as many as 7. I choose 7 when questions are sensitive and I want to give the raters as much room as possible. Other times I will force a positive or a negative answer by using 4 or 3 points. Figure 2.3 forces either a positive or a negative answer; there is not room for a neutural response by the rater.

Whenever scales are built, the purpose for the question and the use of the response need to be considered. Why do you want the person rating an employee to answer in the ways you provide? The answer to that question will help guide the construction of scales.

SUMMARY

This chapter began with a discussion of how program evaluation and performance are different but related. The three ages of performance appraisal were discussed and a system for appraising employees was explored. A hierarchy of evidence that can be used in many settings was reviewed. Finally, important factors in applying performance were reviewed. What is proposed in the next chapter is a system of measurement (and that term is used loosely) that can be understood intuitively by employees. It is based on criterion references (what people do) as opposed to norm references (how people are rated). Chapter 3 provides a step-by-step process that offers a straightforward approach to performance appraisal.

CHAPTER 3

Strategies for Evaluating People

One of the most challenging aspects of management involves evaluating people or performance appraisal. Much of the literature about adults is dedicated to demonstrating that adults have developing egos that partially consist of their performance on the job. People who do performance appraisals should keep that in mind. Whenever someone does a performance appraisal, he or she is involved in examining a person's self, which leads to the term *self-esteem* and all that it brings to mind. Is it any wonder that performance appraisals are dreaded by both employees and supervisors?

Strategies for evaluating people can be viewed as a series of events that involve choosing indicators, setting standards, selecting sources for evidence, recording the evidence, analyzing data, forming conclusions, and making recommendations. These simple steps often involve complex tasks and unintended outcomes. The rest of this chapter looks at these steps in some detail.

CHOOSING THE INDICATORS

Indicators of performance by definition have to be observable. A performance has to be observed before it can be appraised. Indicators should be congruent with a job description or a role definition; they must be linked. Otherwise, the performance appraiser will be guilty of "teaching A and testing B" a complaint some have made about college professors. Managers should state A and compare A. Table 3.1 demonstrates how to

use one item from a role description and turn it into an indicator for use in performance appraisals. The role description presented in Table 3.1 could be for a corporate trainer. It serves as
a platform for the establishment of indicators.

Table 3.1   Role descriptions and indicators

Role description	Indicator
1. Provide individuals, units with training programs related to their needs.	1. Number of programs provided. Number of needs assessments conducted.
2. Keep up-to-date in training methods and subject matter.	2. Number of training programs attended. Number of new methods developed.
3. Conduct evaluations of training programs to determine results and impacts.	3. Number of evaluations conducted. Kinds of impact demonstrated.

Note that each role description item has an indicator that
basically asks if the item has been performed. It could ask how
well it has been done or how often it has been done. If an indicator cannot be written for a role description item, one should
question including it in a job or role description. The best time
to write indicators is when the job description is written. Such
timing improves both documents.

SETTING THE STANDARDS

Once a criterion has been written, the next task is to determine the standards used for the criterion. One point of judgment can have multiple standards. Standards we are most used
to and comfortable with are above average, average, below average, and failing or A, B, C, D, and F. This may be due to the
years we have spent in school where we were judged by these
standards.

I recall being introduced to the bell curve in my early high
school days. Now as a teacher of statistics and research to

graduate students, I still hear the curve referred to as the bell curve. This bell curve or normal distribution is built on standard deviations that tell us how far from average a score is. Schools are slowly changing the way students are judged. Someday in the future the familiar standard will be replaced with other, equally comfortable standards. The cycle needs to be speeded up. We need to become comfortable with a new way of thinking now.

Following is another way to think about how to set standards that are not referenced to all other employees. If the standard of the normal distribution were subscribed to, half of our employees would be condemned to be less than average. No company would tolerate such a situation.

If each person was compared to some criterion that was independent from the average, then it is possible that all employees could meet that standard (or not meet the standard). This means terms such as *totally unacceptable, does not meet expectations, meets expectations, exceeds expectations,* and *extraordinary* need to replace the old more familiar terms.

In one aspect what is proposed is a move from a quantitative assessment to a qualitative one. Quantitative performance appraisals usually involve extensive measurement and produce means and standard deviations. While these statistics may be excellent for describing populations, they do little for describing the performance of one individual.

Qualitative performance appraisal is more description-based and serves well the purpose of helping individuals see their performance in objective terms or at least through the eyes of other people. If qualitative performance appraisal is used, then evaluators and others move away from the notion that half of the employees are required to be below the mean and they move toward a notion that it is possible for everyone to "exceed expectations."

This was brought home to me in a forceful way when a client stated, "Our people want to know what it means to meet expectations." That sounded like a very reasonable question and one that demanded an answer. We worked for two days to define each of the following categories: totally unacceptable, does not meet expectations, meets expectations, exceeds expectations, and extraordinary. I could not give a universal answer to that question because the answer is job-specific. The key was in defining these categories by role description. Our efforts produced a performance appraisal matrix presented in Table 3.2. It can be used in a vertical orientation (reading down the columns) or a horizontal orientation (reading across the rows). The vertical orientation provides a composite picture of five categories of employees from unacceptable to extraordinary. The horizontal orientation provides a profile of all levels of performance possible for a given task. The appendix contains a fully developed personnel evaluation matrix for an adult educator.

The possible varieties of performance in one role description item can be easily seen when using the matrix horizontally. These varieties of performance can be regarded as a continuum on which a person's performance can be located. Employees often want to know what is expected for a certain rating. Using this matrix, a person's performance can be located and the next set of performances can be described and set as a goal.

Using the matrix vertically, an evaluator can determine in a holistic manner what constitutes an excellent (or unacceptable) employee in all job roles.

I am not totally prepared to leave the quantitative field behind. Numbers do play an important part in performance appraisal. Up to this point we have acted as though all role description items carry equal weight. In reality they do not; some are more important than others. This fact can be easily accommodated by weighting the role description items. For example, I know of one continuing education operation where it is more important to secure resources for programs than it is to assess needs. I know of another where the reverse is true. These two units will treat these items differently and will weight them differently.

If the rating categories are valued on a scale from 0 to 4 (totally unacceptable = 0, does not meet expectations = 1, meets expectations = 2, exceeds expectations = 3, and extraordinary = 4), then the role description item weight can be multiplied by the rating category value to produce a number that can be

Table 3.2 A personnel evaluation matrix

Description items	Rating categories				
	Unacceptable	Does not meet expectations	Meets expectations	Exceeds expectations	Extra-ordinary
Provide individuals and units with training programs related to their needs					
Keep up-to-date in training methods and subject matter					
Conduct evaluations of training programs to determine results and impacts					

summed with other values to produce an overall score that is comparable to other employee scores. This provides a ranking that is more objective and defendable than other systems. It is objective because it is based on evidence. It is defendable because it is anchored in behaviors and provides logic to the computations. Any system used should be described to employees before it is implemented, thus giving them targets to shoot for.

SELECTING THE SOURCES

What are the sources of evidence for evaluating people? Job descriptions, other employees, and supervisors are all good sources. A great deal has been said about job descriptions up to this point, so this section will concentrate on the other two sources. "Other employees" refers to asking what other employees think a job should or does entail. Asking "should" questions (What should an employee do?) will produce the ideal type of description. Asking "does" questions (What does an employee do?) will produce a real type of description. The proper route depends on the outcomes desired. If an evaluator desires to improve the job, then he or she should ask for "shoulds." If an actual description is desired then he or she should ask for "does." An evaluator needs to understand clearly the reason for asking one or the other kind of question.

Another source is supervisors. These people are close to the work and know what should and what is being accomplished by the employee. They have a wide range of performances for comparison from former workers who have filled a certain job. The comparative approach is important. Their assessment will be one of the most comprehensive descriptions because of this wide range of comparison points.

Whatever source is used, the data should be gathered in a systematic manner and with an intended end in sight for its use. Systematic approaches include interviews that use a common protocol, questionnaires, and observations. Protocols refer to the questions asked, the way they are asked, and the order in which they are asked. Interviews include all of the items of concern for valid and reliable surveys. The reader is referred to any basic research text that handles these concerns (Frankel & Wallen, 1990; Worthen & Sanders, 1987).

Observations include watching how a job is performed. The observer could be a manager or the employee himself or herself. Observations are aided by use of a checklist that ensures that employees are observed in a standardized manner.

RECORDING THE EVIDENCE

Accomplishments related to job descriptions should be recorded by employees. Such recordings should be comprehensive in nature rather than just a recording of outcomes. Comprehensive recordings provide a broad picture of an individual and her or his accomplishments.

The documentation that an individual prepares as he or she gets ready for the formal appraisal session should be recorded as a person moves throughout a year. One very good way of doing so is to build a portfolio of evidence that supports how well various job description roles are being carried out. In universities and colleges this is referred to as a tenure and promotion file. In other organizations it is known as a personnel file (if the employer keeps it) or an accomplishment file (if the individual keeps it). The portfolio concept will be the focus of this section. This is, incidentally, very close to the notion of portfolio evaluation that is becoming better known than it has been in the past. This kind of evaluation is dynamic and is based with the person being evaluated. The employee builds his or her file from materials naturally occurring on the job. It contains evidence of a person's skills, and the contents will vary depending on the use of the portfolio. For example, if a decision is to be made about a person for a promotion, then the evidence in the portfolio should be targeted toward that decision. Assessment in portfolio evaluation is ongoing and the contents are expected to change over time. Portfolio assessment is a growing new area for evaluation. Questions about portfolio assessment are beginning to be generated and the answers should provide

some confidence in using this form of assessment. Question include: Is this method as reliable as other assessment methods?
and How do employees feel about maintaining records? Some
considerations for using a portfolio system are noted below.

Management should specify the order of the categories
that should be covered by a portfolio. This will provide some
notion of similarity between and among employees who are
being assessed. Otherwise, assessors will have a difficult time
understanding what is being assessed if categories change from
individual to individual. The notion here is not to compare individuals. Instead, the purpose is to help assessors understand
the environment in which the employee works.

For example, suppose that top management in a sales ori-
ented company is responsible for reviewing assessments (not assessing, but reviewing assessments) at the next lower level and
at the level below that one. Suppose also that top management
members are all trained attorneys and understand law very
well, but do not understand sales at all. Here they are being
asked to review the judgments of others regarding tasks with
which they are not familiar. It is a new world for them. Suppose
still further that the assessments and evidence come to them in
different formats stressing different items. Confusion would
reign.

Another example is from higher education. A university's
central administration reviews all promotion and tenure activities and must make some kind of judgment about them. However, the documentation comes from research, teaching, engi-
neering, education, humanities, biology, and other disparate
fields. How can accurate judgments be expected? They can not
be unless there is some commonality within the process. That
commonality can be achieved by asking all candidates to conform to some uniform process. The format should be flexible
enough for people to use in various fields. Role statements provide baselines for judgments to be made.

Evidence is recordable in a number of ways. One way is to
document activities through a narrative. Another way is to collect copies of program outlines, letters of commendation, program evaluation results, newsletters, articles, and monthly reports; these are all excellent ways of recording data.

A second step in recording data is to organize the data so they make sense to a reviewer. Earlier it was argued that a common format should be provided by the reviewers of the file. But how should evidence should be arranged when no specifications are provided? In cases like this, the logic of evidence, or how data should be presented, can come from three sources: the nature of the evidence, the nature of the organization, and the nature of the next possible promotion.

The nature of the evidence should parallel the role description. In turn, the role description should dictate the order and the way the evidence is presented. For example, if my evidence for promotion is mostly videotapes I have produced, then perhaps I should think about using that format in presenting my evidence for promotion. Such a tape would incorporate all of the sound principles of video production with segments from those videos I have produced. However, if most of my evidence included written reports, then I should concentrate on the kind of report the reviewers are used to reading.

The nature of the organization will also have an effect. Suppose I am a continuing educator working in a large research university. Then my evidence for promotion should be presented in a similar way to the university's mission. Research or research-like publications will be featured in my quest for promotion and, in some cases, tenure. The scholarly kinds of work should come first.

If the next possible promotion is to a management or administrative position, then I will want to portray any evidence that will demonstrate I have management potential. This kind of evidence should be highlighted prominently in my file and should come first. Other supporting evidence can come later.

ANALYZING THE DATA

Analyzing the data is related to a part of the preceding steps of defining role statements and specifying how the evidence should be presented. If these steps are done logically and well, then the analysis of data is straightforward and relatively easy.

The number of promotions is limited, and often the amount of dollars that can be used in merit increases is also limited. In other words, a company of 100 employees can not promote all of them at once, nor can it give 10% increases to all of them. The standards used in promotion must be tied to criteria that have been preestablished so that a worker knows what it will take to get a specific rating.

The appendix contains a full schema based on the personnel evaluation matrix presented in Table 3.2. The cells contain data for a rating system within the context of extension work in higher education. The principle is the same for other kinds of work. Criteria must be known by the employee. The job of the performance appraiser is to let employees know how they are doing on those criteria. When criteria are known, then analysis consists of determining how well the evidence matches the criteria. For example, if a criterion states an employee will develop three new programs a year and the evidence shows four were developed, it is an easy matter to know that this person exceeds the expectations of the position.

There should be a system of appeal to other reviewers for employees who feel they have been dealt with unfairly or if they disagree with the assessment. These appeals may be to the next level of management or to a separate assessor.

FORMING CONCLUSIONS

How does one make decisions about promotion once the evidence has been recorded, presented, and analyzed? They are based on the evidence, the same way other decision have been made. One important piece of evidence that is often over looked in promotion situations is the opinion of colleagues. They often have firm opinions about their fellow workers and the quality of their work. It should be up to the employee to present names of colleagues who can give recommendations to a supervisor. It is also important for the supervisor to go beyond the names presented in obtaining comments from colleagues. The employee should know this, and it should be done as part of the evidence-gathering activities.

I have a colleague who carefully reviews the evidence for promotion and then ranks the people he reviews. Some court cases have held this method to be illegal and not a proper way to evaluate employees. While it may be improper for an assessment method, it might be used to validate the conclusion reached by the criterion-based evaluation method discussed above. When such pieces of evidence are assembled, a manager will have a notion of where a particular employee ranks. These data can then be summed (Did they fail to meet, meet, or exceed expectations?) to determine where a person fits in terms of a performance.

MAKING RECOMMENDATIONS

This is where the "rubber meets the road." All of the preceding work is done to make a recommendation about a promotion or a salary increase. This is the act that causes the sweaty palms for both the employee and the supervisor. Remember, the supervisor has to work with this employee for another year. If employees are assessed frequently, they can see a light at the end of the tunnel and will not have to live with an unacceptable label for an entire year. It also prevents the extraordinary people from resting on their laurels for a year and becoming less than they were before the rating.

Such an attitude reflects real life. We do not achieve some pinnacle of success and stay there the rest of our careers. We must achieve and celebrate and then push on to new attainments. A frequent performance appraisal will allow us to do that.

An important strategy in making recommendations is to first make the recommendation to the person being evaluated. An assessor of employees owes it to employees to present his or her findings to them first. In a sense, employees are the assessor's client and they deserve the first look at the results.

Another strategy is for the assessor to ask the employee for reactions to the appraisal. This reaction could even become part of the appraisal; to one degree this is so indicated by the appraisal forms employees are asked to sign. By asking for feedback about conclusions and proposed recommendations, the assessor lets the employee know where he or she stands and what should be accomplished.

Another strategy is to build the recommendations upon the results. For example, if results from a performance appraisal show an employee is lacking is a certain area, then a logical recommendation is for remediation of some kind. On the other hand, if the employee exceeds expectations, it is logical to recognize excellence in some way. Recommendations should be built upon logic.

SUMMARY

This chapter began by discussing role or job descriptions as sources for standards for performance appraisals. Next, a personnel evaluation matrix was described. Sources for performance appraisal were discussed and the observation was made that differing sources will provide not on different levels of validity but also different perspectives on a person. How information or evidence should be recorded was discussed along with ways in which to analyze the information. Making recommendations was discussed in terms of salary and promotions.

CHAPTER 4

Evaluating Programs, Products, and Services

This chapter presents different perspectives that enhance evaluation efforts. A different mind-set is needed when dealing with programs, products, and services than is needed when evaluating people and organizations. Most program, product, or service evaluations deal with how well people like the program, product, or service. In and of itself, this is not bad. However, if an evaluation effort ends here, it misses much of what is important. This chapter begins by describing three models of program evaluation.

THREE MODELS OF PROGRAM EVALUATION

This section does not present a deep review of the selected models of program evaluation, but it does give an overview of how evaluation might be accomplished in three different ways. Each of the models is presented with enough information that it could guide your efforts, and references are provided for those who would like to explore any of the models in added depth. These models have been chosen for two reasons. First, the authors (Eisner, 1975; Guba & Lincoln, 1981; Stufflebeam, 1983) are recognized thinkers in the field of evaluation. Second, these models are among the most often described.

The CIPP Model of Evaluation

Stufflebeam (1983) described the CIPP model as one that can be used to help in decision-making settings. The name of this model comes from four elements of the evaluation process: context, input, process, and product. Each of these elements serves to focus the evaluation questions, and the answers are meant to serve program managers faced with programmatic decisions. Each element is now described in some detail with sample questions from each area.

Context

Context refers to the setting of the program being evaluated. The setting involves the kind of organization sponsoring the program being evaluated, the method and level of funding, and the program staffing patterns within the organization. It is a contextual view of the organization and program. This element of the evaluation can help make sense of findings from the evaluation activity. If an evaluation is like a floodlight on a program, the contextual look at the program is like another floodlight on the scene.

Questions that this element or phase of evaluation can address include: What need is the program intended to meet? How was the planning done or how is it being done? (The CIPP model can be used in a formative sense as well as a summative one.) Who is the target population? Are the objectives appropriate given the needs of the target population?

Findings from the evaluation may very well include some notion about the adequacy of the program context. Information from this element can help decision makers focus on aspects that are not necessarily part of the program, but that do affect the program and its outcomes.

Input

Input refers to the resources available to and used by the program in meeting its goals. Resources can be defined as time, dollars, people, expertise, volunteers, and strategies for obtaining the outcomes. The major question to ask here is, "Were (or are) the resources sufficient to meet the objectives of the program?" Other related questions include: Does the program have access to the expertise needed to accomplish the goals? What is lacking? Are there other ways of meeting the goals? Are they being used? Why or why not?

Answers to these questions will affect the final report. It becomes another anchor point for the judgments made about a program. It is yet another floodlight on the scene.

Process

Process deals with how well the program was implemented. Sometimes a program is excellent as written out or described on paper. However, when it comes to implementation, it is another matter. Recently I was involved in a national evaluation for a major educational publishing house that sold a curriculum to a number of school districts across the nation. The company wanted a group of us to determine the differences their curriculum made in learners. We found few differences because of the curriculum. However, we also found the curriculum was not well implemented. In the best implementing site, school officials were following the implementation guides at about a 50% level. Therefore, it was not surprising there were no differences. In effect, the program did not exist.

Questions to ask at this level include: How well is the plan being implemented? What changes should be made? Is the implementation different from what was planned? Why?

Findings from these questions will do two things. First, they allow the evaluator to discover what problems may exist if there are no differences because of the program. This failure to implement is a large cause of problems for education, management, and training. Too often a company will hire an outside training consultant and then fail to insist that the company goals or outcomes drive the program, relying instead on the consultant's "canned" goals to drive the program.

Second, findings from these questions make this area of inquiry one of the most important for a formative evaluation. It is this area that produces excellent suggestions for change.

Product

Product refers to the outcomes from a program. Product here can be thought of in more than the usual sense of objects. It also includes skills, attitudes, or knowledge. Questions of how much, what quality, and timing are asked. Judgments become the natural outcome from this section.

The CIPP model offers different perspectives of a program under review. It is a thorough look at a program from its contexts to its outcomes. It is built upon knowing ahead of time what the program objectives are and what needs a program is designed to meet. It is a detached (objective) look at accomplishments. The next model presented takes a different approach in that it does not assume an evaluator can know what the objectives are for a program. Participants in a program often bring their own personal objectives with them, and these may differ from the stated program goals and may even differ from one person to another.

The Naturalistic Model

Guba and Lincoln (1981) provided the field of evaluation with a different perspective. One of the fundamental differences between evaluation efforts in this model and others is the basic philosophical orientation of the evaluators. This model does not rely exclusively on statistics and science. Instead, this model relys on the views of the individuals participating in the program as a holistic picture of what is meaningful to participants. The traditional concerns of validity, reliability, and objectivity are replaced by concerns of credibility, fit, auditability, and confirmability. Each of these elements of a good naturalistic evaluation are achieved in various ways. Credibility is achieved by looking at a program or evaluation object from different perspectives. Some have termed this *triangulation*; however, triangulation refers to using widely divergent approaches to a problem. For example, if a person were to both measure and engage in naturalistic evaluation, credibility would be much greater than to merely survey two different populations or to interview two different groups of people.

Fit is achieved by using a thick description, which means many pages of narrative that fully explain the program or project or product. This is done so that people who read about the evaluation will understand more completely when the findings of studies apply and when they do not. Naturalistic evaluations use the methods of anthropology and ethnology, which are basically observation methods.

Auditability is achieved by providing a trail of evidence for other evaluators to follow. In fact, a good tactic is to ask a second team to follow the same evidence trail (audit trail) as a first team and see if similar conclusions are reached. This assumes that naturalistic evaluators keep transcripts, tapes, and other evidence for others to follow. This is related to the remaining element of confirmability. Confirmable data help others understand the factual nature of the evaluations performed.

One final note regarding naturalistic evaluation deals with its methods. Many evaluators falsely believe that if qualitative methods (interviews, case studies, ethnographies, and the like) are used, they are engaged in naturalistic inquiry. The most important element that makes a study naturalistic or otherwise is the role the questions or hypotheses play in the study. If the evaluator leaves his or her baggage at the door and has no preconceived notion as to what is or is not, then the evaluator is engaged in naturalistic evaluation. If, on the hand, the investigator has questions or hypotheses in mind and begins exploring to answer those questions, he or she is engaged in nonnaturalistic inquiry. Depending upon how rigorous and systematic a person is, he or she may actually be doing science.

Connoisseurship Model

Art is interesting to some people and disturbing to others because the observer or viewer of art brings his or her interpretation to the object. And so it is with the connoisseurship model of evaluation. There are no hard and fast rules to adhere to, no specific and descriptive explanation of how to value, and no step-by-step process to follow. The evaluation process is centered in the evaluator, just as art criticism is centered in the connoisseur of art.

Eisner (1975), who has spend much of his time in art education, has provided an evaluation model built on connoisseurship and criticism. The roots in art are obvious. The evaluator is an expert who is in effect the instrument or measuring device. The appreciation of educational programs is so complex (much like art) that an expert is needed to make judgments about the merit and worth of a program. It is the expert who values the program or object of evaluation. This means the evaluator has broad and extensive experience in the area or project being evaluated. Eisner compares this type of evaluation with wine tasting. There are many elements that make a wine excellent. The connoisseur of wine understands and has had experience with each one. So too, the evaluator operating in this model understands and appreciates the many elements of the program being evaluated. This understanding and appreciation is built on extensive experience with the evaluation object.

The model is not a stepwise progression; instead, all elements are detected by the evaluator at the correct time according to the expert. If an evaluator were to use this model and did not have the expertise assumed by the model, then he or she would have to contract for an expert.

The other element of this model is the criticism of a program or some other evaluation object. Making the judgments of the expert known is practicing the art of criticism. This is where the value of the program is made known to others. Just as the case of the art critic, the education, management, or training critic does not provide the methods used to arrive at the conclusions. Examples may be given and reasons for the judgment may be offered. However, just as an art critic, the evaluator as critic is respected (and sometimes feared) because of his or her reputation and insights.

Criticism involves lifting people so they appreciate the object that is before them. In evaluation this means helping people appreciate what is being studied. Limitations and problems may well be pointed out. This model is intuitive and is best learned by apprenticeship to an expert.

I once conducted an evaluation of a set of syllabi used at the university level of study in a humanities area. I know little of the humanities and what should be taught there. I contracted with a nationally known expert to comment on the documents. His insights were valuable to the report. On the basis of his years of experience and his broad exposure to the field of humanities education, this person was able to offer insight and criticism of the documents.

However, this was only one part of a larger report. We also reported the numbers of students involved, their reactions to the courses, and faculty responses to the project. The connoisseurship model was used as part of a larger study and did not stand on its own. I like using it in conduction with other models such as the CIPP model where connoisseurship makes sense in terms of product.

EVALUATING PROGRAM PLANNING

In this section, program evaluation will be considered from a different perspective—before a program is put in place. The three models just considered lend themselves well to evaluating programs that have been in place for a time. But what of those programs that are about to be implemented or have been in place for only a short time? In these situations evaluability assessment is a useful tool.

One of the problems with programs of any type is that initially they may be poorly designed. Someone (a manager) may come in with a proposal to train employees when that is not what is needed. For example, suppose that attitudes about safety rules need to be changed and a training program is designed to deliver lectures. Has it ever been possible to change someone's attitude by lecturing to them? It doesn't work. What does? That is a question for an instructional designer or a competent trainer. The issue here is, how does an evaluator know if the lack of results was due to poor program planning or instructional design?

These problems can be detected by evaluability assessment, which refers to what can be called program planning audits. Planning audits can be done before a program takes place, during a program, or after a program has been carried out. Planning audits were originally designed to avoid costly evaluation on large-scale programs where no results would turn up because a program was thought to exist, but in reality did not. It asks the question, "Is there anything here to evaluate?" The steps are relatively easy to follow. While evaluators may not want to do a full-fledged evaluability assessment, they certainly will want to be aware of the answers to important questions asked in doing an evaluability assessment.

Smith (1989) provided a detailed description of 10 steps involved in evaluability assessments. While it is not our purpose to provide the depth she gives in her book, the steps will be reviewed briefly so that a program planning audit process can be implemented as programs are examined. A school-age child care (SACC) program will be used as an example in the following steps.

Task 1: Determine Purpose, Secure Commitment, and Identify Audit Work Group Members

Any look at a program will take time and resources. Commitments to the activity provide the evaluator with a needed perspective about what is realistically expected by management. A member of the top management, preferably a vice president from the corporate office, should be a part of the work group in order to supply continued support and an understanding of what the study is about. Determining the purpose will limit what the audit is about and how deeply it will examine issues. The audit group is a working group and members will be involved for a number of days. An audit group should be appointed by the CEO of an organization, a charge should be given, and a scope of work should be outlined.

Task 2: Define Boundaries of the Program to be Audited

Some programs that are not well thought out are fuzzy around the edges. This boundary establishment is important. It helps define the program and limit its expected effects. All too often in planning, adult educators, trainers, and others hang extra expectations on a program. The boundaries of a program can be geographical or functional (having to do with goals, services, etc.). For example, the team should formally state that this project will examine the SACC project in Adams County.

Task 3: Identify and Analyze Program Documents

This task is meant to establish program rhetoric. In other words, the evaluator is trying to determine what the program is about from those who are in charge of the program. It is a look at the history of a program. Many times important decisions are made before evaluation begins, and this is an attempt to understand those past decisions. It also gives the investigator an idea of what has gone on before. For example, proposals for the SACC program, brochures or flyers sent to parents, and annual reports could be examined.

Task 4: Develop/Clarify Program Theory

This is perhaps the most complex task outlined by Smith (1989) and is the task that has the most serious implications for adult educators and trainers. This task is more or less a "proving" of the developed programs. Smith noted that in this task, assumptions of the program are examined as well as statements about how and why a program is supposed to work. Any gaps in the logic or the theory are examined. This step provides the logic for believing that the specified outcomes will be a result of the program as described. When these beliefs are written out, they form a logic model and make the program theory clear. For example, reading tutorials are provided in the SACC program and there is a stated outcome that reading levels will be improved. There is a logic present.

Task 5: Identify and Interview Stakeholders

This critical task involves talking with stakeholders who have an interest in a program. These people are defined as either program funders, participants, or providers. Their opinions about what the program should deliver and is delivering is important to the continuation of any program whether it be one in business, industry, government, or education. These people have influence on the program and are essential to its future. Smith noted this task is designed to get information from stakeholders and not to provide information to them. For example, SACC stakeholders include the district superintendent, school principal, schoolteachers, parents, social workers, public safety officials, and child welfare officials.

Task 6: Describe Shareholder Perceptions of Program

A description of stakeholder perceptions can be done a number of ways. A narrative of the program can be written or a presentation of the program can be made in terms of the models created in the above examples. A combination of narrative and models would most fully describe perceptions about the program. For example, focus group interviews and individual interview results are reported.

Task 7: Identify Stakeholder Needs, Concerns, and Differences in Perceptions

Differences in perceptions can be identified by comparing stakeholder perceptions to the program logic model developed in Task 4. When differences appear between the model and expectations, the reasons for the differences need to be explored. The first seven tasks provide an idea as to whether a program actually exists and if the program is meeting or is designed to meet stakeholder expectations. For example, some stakeholders may see the need to keep school-age children occupied until working parents can care for them; others may see the need for increased academic instruction. The logic model should address both. If it does not, then a gap exists.

Task 8: Determine Plausibility of Program Model

This task is accomplished by determining if program goals are defined, if the program to reach those goals is defined, if there are sufficient and appropriate activities to meet the goals, and if there are sufficient resources to support the activities. For example, the gaps noted in the preceding step indicate there may not be an adequate program to address reported needs.

Task 9: Draw Conclusions and Make Recommendations

Even though conclusions are made in all auditing tasks, this is the time when those subconclusions are summarized and the entire process is considered. The purposes of the audit are examined and the conclusions are drawn in consideration of those purposes. For example, if the purpose of a particular study was to improve a program, then the conclusions should be made in that context. For example, in the SACC analysis the report might state the safety and welfare officials thought it should offer constructive use of time, but the program made little or no effort in this area. There was an oversight on the part of the program developers.

Task 10: Plan Specific Steps for Utilization of Evaluability Assessment Data

While this is the last task presented, in reality it is considered throughout the evaluability assessment process. The involvement of decision makers within the stakeholder group will help this task come to reality. In a sense it is the evaluator's last chance to see something come from his or her efforts. An action plan should be developed for use by the decision makers. Evaluators can ask for a follow-up meeting some time in the future in order to provide a sense of accountability for the use of the results. For example, SACC may well involve ignored officials in the next round of program development. Because the superintendent's office was involved at the outset, it is likely such bridges will be built.

PRODUCT EVALUATION

Scriven (1981) produced an excellent set of questions that can guide an evaluator in product assessment. He noted that a product must be thought about and evaluated in terms of its actual function and not in terms of desired or the intended function. The first question asks, "What are the desirable qualities that this product should have?" The question serves as a focus for the following ones. It becomes an important question because standards are being set with the answers to the question.

The second question is, "What resources do I have to obtain, maintain, or improve the product?" Related questions include: "What will it take to keep the product going?" "What investments in terms of time and money will it take?" Answers to these questions will demonstrate a company's ability to support products.

The third question is, "What solutions are possible given the needs and available resources?" This question will limit the field of consideration. Scriven used several examples to show that competing products should be considered more less in a head-to-head competition. He did not limit competitors to the same kind of product. For example, he told a story of how two very different products (a mirror and an elevator) were competitors for the same solution. The solution was lack of adequate elevator service in a large building. More elevators were proposed as the solution (a very expensive one), but the installation of a large mirror (a relatively inexpensive solution) next to the existing elevator helped people "reflect" about other things than the time they were spending waiting for the elevator.

The fourth question is, "Which products have the needed qualities?" The methods of the *Consumer Reports* magazine are an example of how this can be determined where important qualities of a product are judged as "much better than average," "better than average," "average," "below average," or "much below average."

The fifth question asks, "What other capabilities or flaws does the product have?" Many products can do multiple jobs. The personal computer is a good example of this. Someone buying a computer as a word processor would be ill advised to use that as the only judgment criteria because a computer can do a number of different tasks. Other examples are training films that have multiple uses and structured exercises that have many applications. Scriven proposed that these other functions can be useful in judging products.

The sixth question has to do with costs: "What will a product cost not only for acquisition, but also for maintenance?" An important cost in today's world of exploding knowledge is life expectancy and replacement costs.

The seventh question is built on information from the preceding questions: "What is the best buy?" All data collected and analyzed according to the answers to the first six questions are now brought into play to answer this crowning question.

These questions apply to diverse products such as software, books, videotapes, and training programs. It might be useful at this point to quickly review the questions with one of these kinds of products in mind. For example, I had a training director ask me about a program for problem-solving skills. She was choosing between two competitors. By using the questions above, she soon learned that the products she thought were similar were actually quite different.

What desirable qualities should this product have? My friend noted that desirable qualities for a training program would be effectiveness, portability, and the ability to start training on a moment's notice. These qualities may be different for different situations, but for her company's needs, these were important at this time.

What resources do I have to obtain, maintain, or improve the product? She began to think about the future. Would she have to call an outside consultant every time training was needed? Or, could she develop the training capability within her staff? One of the programs was proprietary; the other was not. This became an important question for her to answer.

What solutions are possible given the needs and available resources? The training director began to think about other possible solutions that did not include training as it is usually thought about. One of the solutions she considered was using strategically placed instructional cards that employees could read as the need arose. However, because the problem was one of lack of skills, she choose a skill-oriented training program.

Which products have the needed qualities? This question allowed her to narrow the possible solutions, not only to skill-oriented training programs but among training programs. Those programs that did not built future training capacity within her organization were eliminated.

What other capabilities or flaws does the product have? My friend considered what effects a skill training program would have on morale, trust, communication, group effectiveness, and problem solving. While these capabilities may not be centrally important, they were additions that helped her make a selection among several training programs.

What will a product cost, not only for acquisition but also for maintenance? She began to think about the issue of transfer from the training session to application on the job. One of the programs made a definite point about transfer to on-the-job problems and to continued reinforcement for newly learned skills.

What is the best buy? After considering the first six questions, the answer to this question was a face-to-face training program that emphasized skill acquisition and that featured building capabilities within company training staff for follow-up.

If deeper looks at what should be evaluated are taken, then some of the problems associated with shallow evaluations can be avoided. I know of one distance learning program where for years the evaluations were always positive. When a deeper analysis was performed, however, the data showed that the learners were positive about the opportunities to learn. Actually, they were quite negative about the system, the learning materials, and the support services provided to them. Care must be taken by administrators, managers, and evaluators to examine carefully what is being evaluated and what the results mean. The preceding six questions allow a careful examination of products, and a careful analysis will produce useful and safe decisions.

EVALUATING TRAINING SERVICES

Many companies spend thousands of dollars in training workers, both managers and hourly employees as well as boards of directors and other staff members. This investment is huge. Recently I was asked to address the issue of evaluating training and development activities at a meeting of trainers, chief executive officers (CEOs), and others from across the United States. My message was not very optimistic because of two reasons. First, but not most difficult, is the fact that it is hard to measure training outcomes and relate those to dollar amounts. Second, and most troublesome, companies do not seem willing to pay for good evidence that training works. These two problems need to be considered.

One reason it is difficult to evaluate results from training programs is that often there is an absence of baseline data to use for comparison purposes. If the baseline information exists, it is usually so far removed from the training outcomes that too many other factors can interfere with outcomes and measures. Baseline information refers to how an organization is doing in selected areas. For example, the number of widgets produced in an hour on an assembly line is a baseline number, as is sick days taken, number of customer complaints, company morale (as measured by a survey), and almost any other indicator you can think of. What makes something "baseline" is the fact that it has been collected for sometime and that it is used for before and after comparisons.

This is not a research text, but in a sense this is about research. Some readings are taken before the experiment (or training, or intervention), the experiment (or training, or intervention) is done, and then readings are taken afterward. The important thing to realize is that some comparison data are available before the training begins. If a sound needs assessment was done before the training was designed, then baseline data may already exist in some form. Reports that were independent from a needs assessment may also provide baseline data.

If management requires data on the effectiveness of training, then the trainer must be willing to find the baseline data and use it in demonstrating training effectiveness. This leads to the second reason for pessimism in validating training effectiveness. Management is often unwilling to pay the expense of collecting such data either before or after training. They often ask for the famous "bottom line" when no top line exists.

To overcome this problem, the evaluator or trainer/evaluator should look for the best evidence. This will not constitute proof that a training program works, but it will supply good evidence that it does.

One example is a large firm (7,000 employees) that had invested thousands of dollars in an external training program (one supplied by people from outside the company). Company officials wanted to know what effects the program was having on the firm. There were no baseline data as is usually the case, so an evaluator was contracted to prove the results. He diligently produced a competent design that would provide valid results. The company officials balked at the price of the evaluation and cut it off soon after he began the study. The training program in question built skills in problem solving for participants who were from various divisions of the firm and who did not ordinarily interact with one another. Sometime after the training session ended, this same group of participants called itself together. They selected a recurring multimillion dollar problem the company faced and decided to correct the problem using the skills taught at the training program. They were successful.

It seems to me that the best evidence would demonstrate the value of this training program, even though it would not stand as a valid research study. Logic can and should play a large part in evaluating human resource development (HRD) programs.

Framework for Judging Training Programs

The framework presented below is not a presentation of instruments or quick fixes. Too often management asks training departments for quick fixes, and just as often trainers ask evaluators for quick fixes. There are no quick and easy ways for evaluators to do their jobs. Numerous requests have been made for a generic evaluation instrument (one that can fit all situations). A generic evaluation will provide generic results from which generic conclusions can be made and generic recommendations offered.

Evaluations must be grounded in objectives, contexts, and individuals. To do otherwise is folly. The framework spoken of earlier is a guide to looking at the right things for the right reasons. It is intended to operate at an abstract level so that its can be applied to a variety of settings. The framework is based on the work of Smith (1991) of the University of Maryland and of Mueller (1991) of the University of Minnesota. The framework is based on the assumption that an excellent training program should have relevance, quality, and commitment.

Relevance

Programs that are excellent address important organizational problems. The problems are clearly understood by stakeholders, and they understand the extent to which they affect the organization. If any of the elements—importance, clarity, and extent—are missing, then the training program may not be a relevant one, and thus by definition not an excellent one. This implies there are data about the extent of the problem within the organization. Problem indicators are known. (If they are not, then how can anyone expect HRD to provide information about its impact on the problem?) Excellent programs use other existing organizational efforts to help remedy the problem. Smith (1991) suggested the following five questions be asked to help determine if a program is *relevant*.

1. Is the need met by means other than training? Mager (1970) told the story of a manager wanting a training program in order to increase sales of strawberry ice cream because chocolate and vanilla outsold strawberry by twice as much. Further investigation showed that chocolate and vanilla had twice the sales commission. It was an incentive problem, not a training problem. Other solutions include providing information as contrasted with developing skills.

2. Have others who have an interest in the problem and its solution been involved? Recently a colleague and I proposed a solution to an employee assessment problem. We thought the current assessment program was not meeting the needs of management. However, when we talked with those who supposedly had the problem, it really did not exist. Often, one group of people thinks another group of people have a

problem when they don't, or the problem is different from what it was first thought it to be.

3. What are the characteristics of the situation? What are the numbers involved? These become the baseline data mentioned earlier.

4. Is the potential program part of the organization's priorities? If the training program cannot be related to an organization's reasons for being, then it is likely not a good idea to become involved with a proposed program.

5. Is the timing right? Will the problem likely go away if nothing is done? Will it get worse? Is the problem just beginning?

All of these questions have to do with relevance. Smith recommended that these questions be asked primarily before a program takes place.

Quality

Muller (1991) noted that "quality means results" (p. 13). Results are based on problem selection, commitment, implementation, and program review.

Smith (1991) asked several questions in an effort to determine quality. First, Do the people involved in the training have the necessary competencies to carry out the program? These competencies include technical as well as training competencies. Smith noted the time to answer this question is during and before the event.

Second, Is the proposed program plausible and can the outcomes be measured? Plausible means that outcomes have been identified that are clear and that focus on use. Instructional techniques have been selected on the basis of the kinds of outcomes desired. Another consideration is the adequacy of resources for the program. Have enough resources been allocated to make the program work? Yet another element that will make a program plausible is the identification of performance indicators for both individual participants and the program itself.

Other quality issues include efficient use of resources, evidence of goal achievement, and evidence of client satisfaction. Efficient use of resources means that time, money, and materials, are well used by attendees. At how many training programs are handouts given out, only to be discarded as soon as participants are out the door? Worse yet, in how many cases are the feelings or skills acquired during the program lapse not practiced or even attempted to be implemented in the workplace?

Evidence of goal achievement means that indicators have to be selected that reflect implementation of skills. Evidence of client satisfaction is relatively easy to obtain, but collection of such measures is often ill timed. At the close of many training programs, opinionnaires are distributed that ask how satisfied participants are and how likely it is that they will implement a skill. In the sense of achieving an accurate reading, a better time for distributing opinionnaires would be a month or two later when participants have had a chance to implement the skills or otherwise use the intended outcomes.

Smith's third and final criteria for program excellence is utility (see also Patton, 1982). Smith called for evidence that the target audience used the results in some way. Evidence could include a change in the problem or need that prompted the program. Another aspect of this element is the numbers of people involved. If a program can demonstrate these elements, then a judgment can be made about its quality.

Commitment

Programs that are excellent make a commitment of resources that are timely and time-bound. Excellent training programs anticipant training problems or respond to them in a timely way. Trainers make a commitment to solving a problem within a time limit. There is no open-ended stance. Resources are adequate to meet the challenge presented by problems. The training function has the capacity to deliver the program needed.

Commitment reflects more than just availability of personnel. It also means the availability of materials, the means to travel, the commitment of time, and the agreement of the CEO that such training is needed. For example, I have been involved in meetings where training has been judged as important, but there has been a high level of reluctance to let people leave their home station to attend needed training activities.

Commitment means putting the resources in line with the rhetoric of an organization. No program can be excellent unless there is a sufficient level of commitment.

SUMMARY

This chapter presented three models for evaluation. Each model is quite different from the others, but each can be used in conjunction with the others. Evaluating the planning of programs before activities actually take place was also considered. Because many programs produce products, how products can be evaluated was also discussed. Finally, the outcomes of training programs were considered along with a framework for judging training programs.

CHAPTER 5

Strategies for Evaluating Programs, Products, and Services

Before considering ways to evaluate programs, the term *program* needs to be defined. This discussion could have appropriately taken place in chapter 4. It takes place here to illustrate how closely linked indicators, strategies, and methods are with the way we think about programs and goals.

Program is a term used widely in the fields of evaluation, training, and adult education. It is a term that has never been defined in such a way that it consistently means the same thing to various readers. A definition of program is not carried from one context to another. I understand the term *program* to mean a series of events or activities that lead people to a goal. A colleague uses the term to mean one activity that could last a few hours. To him, a program can be a meeting of professionals for the purpose of updating knowledge, and that may take only a half day. Another colleague uses the term to mean helping people buy affordable housing, a program that contains many different kinds of activities and involves numerous days.

Next there is the issue of objectives. Program objectives are different from learning objectives. For example, the affordable housing program mentioned above has as its objective the purchase of housing by people who cannot normally afford housing and thus are living in rented facilities. The program goal is not stated in terms of the changed performance of participants due to learning, although along the way they will learn and change behavior. Program goals are stated in terms of broader affects. For example, a program goal associated with low-income families and housing may be stated as such: The

Low Income Housing Program will enable individuals below an annual income of $25,000 to qualify for housing loans. Or, 20% of the participants in the Low Income Housing Program will qualify for housing after implementing skills learned in the program. These kinds of goals contrast with learning objectives such as "participants will calculate their annual income from all sources." In terms of program goals, we can say that they will mostly refer to a changed state of affairs while learning goals or instructional objectives usually refer to learned capabilities. In terms of Bennette's hierarchy (see chapter 2), program goals are usually expressed at levels 6 and 7 while learning goals are expressed at level 5.

Strategies vary widely and are dependent on the context of the evaluation. The object of the evaluation also affects the kinds of strategies used. This chapter presents various strategies within the elements of conducting an evaluation: choosing the indicators, setting the standards, selecting the sources, recording the evidence, analyzing the data, forming conclusions, and making recommendations. Because these elements are similar whether one is evaluating programs, services, or products, the following discussion applies to all three evaluation objects.

CHOOSING THE INDICATORS

Indicators are important in determining the success of a program, product, or service. They are the crucial to the development of evaluation because without indicators, there are no means by which evaluation can take place. Functioning without indicators would be similar to playing a game without a goal. Imagine playing a basketball game without baskets.

Indicators are not arbitrary things. They are not selected on a whim or in a last minute rush to do evaluation. Indicators are selected before much of the planning takes place. They are moved into the spotlight early in thinking about programs, products, or services. Once I was asked to help determine if a food processing plant should be located in a rural area. The potential investors had set a certain level of raw materials needed for the plant to be cost-effective. I asked the stakeholders what they would accept as indicators. Their response was survey results that asked agricultural producers about the likelihood of them selling their crops to the plant at given price levels.

Indicators come from the results of needs analysis. They are easily found in the results of surveys, public meetings, social indicators, and the like that are part of need analyses. Whenever needs analyses are done, indicators can be found. Conceptually, needs analysis is closely related to evaluation. In fact, many evaluation courses have sections dealing with needs analysis (Witken, 1984).

Another source of indicators (and this source provides more refined indicators) is program objectives. If an objective is well written, it should contain not only the indicator but also a standard (see the following section for a discussion of standards). These will likely be stated in measurable terms and be readily available for use. Actually, well-written objectives need few changes to turn them into usable indicators. The objective for the Low Income Housing Program discussed above can be used as an example. It contains an indicator of program success: qualification for a housing loan. It also contains the standard: 20% of participants with incomes below $25,000. Other standards could be included in the indicator (for example, time involved, the cost of housing qualified for, and so forth).

Often an evaluator will encounter a program that has few if any articulated objectives. Some programs are not fully implemented and offer no guidance. What should be done? A recent experience I had with evaluating services may give an answer.

Our evaluation team conducted an evaluation of quality circles. First, we met a supervisor and one other employee and came away with a sense that they were puzzled about what needed to be looked at. Later, we met with about 20 individuals who were involved in one way or another. We wanted to find out what was important to know and what questions they would like answered. Our team agreed on a strategy we thought would help indicators come to the surface. This was difficult because they were not sure about what questions should be asked. Besides, there were some feelings of an inter-personal nature; the employees did not want to damage relationships with one another.

We passed out a sheet of paper to each person and asked them to write two questions they would like answered about their situation. One was a public question they did not mind the group discussing. The second was a private question they did not care to have discussed. We retained these private questions for our team to discuss and to build a process for the answering of both types of questions. It was interesting to note that most of the private questions were also submitted as public questions by others in the group. We freely discussed almost all of the questions.

Another strategy for building indicators is to ask, "What do you want to know, and what will you accept as evidence for any claims that are made?" This question can be asked of various stakeholder groups. The evaluator should be prepared for different answers. Some work will be needed to resolve conflicting needs for evidence. Most people to do not think of evaluation indicators in such simplistic terms, but in reality indicators do equal evidence.

Yet another strategy for building indicators is to review written reports or other published documents. Not only does this provide an understanding of corporate culture, but it also lets the evaluator know what is valued by a company or an individual. An astute evaluator can report indicators in terms the company values and understands.

These strategies can modify and polish the fundamental indicators found in program objectives. They do not replace them, however.

SETTING THE STANDARDS

The issue of setting standards revolves around working with stakeholders and the objectives of the program, purposes of the product, or outcome of the service. Some objectives, probably the majority, will not include the notion of standards.

If this is the case, the evaluator works with stakeholders to determine acceptable standards.

Standards refer to how much of an objective, purpose, or outcome is obtained. For example, will 20% of participants achieving an objective be good enough for program success? Will 50%, or will 95%, or are there some circumstances where 100% must be the standard? Examples can be found for each standard. Standards are not something we arbitrarily set and then move on to other tasks. Thought must go into this activity. What objective could possibly have 100% as a standard? Or 20% as a standard? It would not be acceptable if only 20% of physicians learning a new surgical technique successfully completed a professional continuing education program. However, 20% of low income families qualifying for housing loans would likely be a grand success. Standards in this sense are situational and depend entirely on a number of factors. These factors include: effects on people who do not participate in a program as in the case of the continuing medical education example above, barriers that may prohibit success in achieving the goal as in the low income housing example, and willingness of stakeholders to accept certain levels of success. This last factor is a political one. Some stakeholders may not be as sensitive about standards as others, and that sensitivity may change over time.

Suppose an evaluator has been asked to evaluate a program funded by tax dollars in an election year. Suppose also that one of the stakeholders is an elected official. Anyone would dare guess that the standards would be higher than they would be after the election. Also, the same may hold for a director of an HRD program in a business that is facing some cutbacks in programs. Standards are relative to conditions and contexts.

Evaluators do not set standards; they work with stakeholders in doing so. Otherwise, the evaluator rather than the stakeholder pronounces success or failure. Evaluators' roles are to bring the stakeholder to the point of setting standards. Some ways of doing this involve private meetings with evaluator contractors.

I recently was asked to help set standards for a large unified school district. My contact from the district knew what he wanted as standards, but parents became aware of the evaluation and wanted to help set the standards. One private meeting turned out to be several focus groups with parents concerning the level of services supplied by the district.

SELECTING THE SOURCES

Indicators and evidence come from many sources. The problem is finding or getting to the right sources with the right questions. Stakeholders and the nature of the questions are guides to finding the sources. This is one reason the use of an advisory committee is so important. They can not only help select the sources of information, but in many instances they can provide access to those sources. Sometimes an evaluator must co-opt an informal advisory board member. Recently I met with a dean from a community college where we were evaluating a faculty evaluation system. We had no advisory group for this study, but he was our contact with the college. We informed him of what we are doing and relied on him for making the needed contacts at the college. His administrative assistant was most helpful and became an informal member of our team.

Sources of data include things like people, records, and publications. People are varied in their perspectives and understanding of the program or product being evaluated. For example, a user of a product will have a different perspective about it than will a supervisor of the individual using the product. If an employee is using a self-study manual to improve his abilities to do the job, his supervisor's impression might include observations about the amount of time taken from the job to use the manual. The supervisor could not comment on the readability of the manual or the accuracy of information in the manual. The supervisor could comment on any improvement noticed in performing the job.

An employee using the manual could comment on all of the issues mentioned above, plus she could tell the evaluator whether she preferred learning on her own or if she preferred learning with other learners. Different sources will give different perspectives on issues.

Records and publications are useful sources of information because they give historical perspectives, official positions, and sometimes controversial debates. I remember looking at the minutes of a university committee meeting and reading how a faculty member was taken to task by his colleagues over an issue of quality. The language was strong and the implications were plain. Publications also provide an understanding of the rhetoric of a program. They often provide an outlook on the program as it should be under ideal circumstances.

Some sources are better than others. What makes them so? It is the issue of believability. Is the source credible? Does the source have the needed information? Also, is the source respected by the people who will be reading or hearing the evaluation report?

RECORDING THE EVIDENCE

Recording the evidence is perhaps the area given most attention by evaluators, with good reason. This is how evaluation data are gathered. This is where most people think the work of evaluation occurs. Recording the evidence involves building instruments, protocols, and evaluation design. In a way it is the coming together of all the other points discussed thus far in this chapter.

Building the instruments involves an understanding of biased language, brevity and coverage, and readability. These concepts are undergirded by a much simpler concept and one that most can relate to. Instruments should be kept simple, easy, and interesting. How is this done? Some examples follow.

Keeping instruments simple means they should be fairly straightforward. If a study is about the effectiveness of a human resource development program (training), then it is imperative that the first questions asked on an instrument deal with the subject at hand. To researchers this is known as face validity. Many instruments lose an individual when they begin to stray from the topic of the instrument. If evaluators are interested in a subject, their instruments must reflect that interest.

Instruments should have a look about them that communicates professionalism. I once received a questionnaire that was printed on tissue-like paper. It was very thin and appeared to be less than a professional approach to the question. This same questionnaire had many difficult items to which I was supposed to respond. It took too long for me to figure out, so I used my time most efficiently and disposed of it. Thoughtful use of white space is important. By not crowding too much on a page and by paying careful attention to the way questions are laid out, the evaluator can use many questions in small space. The questionnaire that uses the same scale can be changed from the example in the following figure (see Figure 5.1) to the one in the succeeding figure (see Figure 5.2).

In the second example, four questions are asked rather than two and they are asked in two fewer lines. Additionally, the white space gives a feeling of openness and an easier response mechanism. When there are many questions to ask or when one stem can be used with modified responses or adjectives, then many opportunities for saving space appear.

Biased language is some times difficult to spot, especially in one's own work. One way to test for bias is to ask a colleague to read for questions that tend to present only one side of an issue. I was recently involved in an evaluation of a school district that focused on a controversial issue. Parents and teachers had strong feelings on both sides of the issue. We created an advisory board with representatives of both sides of the issue and had them look at the items we built. Their comments and suggestions were most helpful, and after responding to their concerns, we felt confident we had as unbiased an instrument as possible. In fact, advisory board members from both sides of the issue became great defenders of the evaluation.

Biased language is a difficult thing to deal with because evaluators are so close to it that they cannot often see it themselves. For example, the following question and scale is biased:

How important do you think world peace is?

Very important, Important, Somewhat important, or Not important.

The scale provides three classifications of importance and

1.	I think that the causes of war are less prevalent in the world today than they were two years ago.			
1. Strongly Disagree	2. Disagree	3. Undecided	4. Agree	5. Strongly Disagree
2.	The United States should provide economic aid to the newly formed republics in Eastern Europe.			
1. Strongly Disagree	2. Disagree	3. Undecided	4. Agree	5. Strongly Disagree

Figure 5.1 Inefficient question layout

* * *

How often do you seek assistance in keeping, interpreting or using the following financial records or documents?

Cash Receipts	Never	Seldom	Sometimes	Frequently	Always
Cash Expenses	Never	Seldom	Sometimes	Frequently	Always
Employee Records	Never	Seldom	Sometimes	Frequently	Always
Balance Sheets	Never	Seldom	Sometimes	Frequently	Always

Figure 5.2 Efficient question layout

only one of unimportance. The results from the survey will naturally be biased toward importance.

A word of caution and consolation is appropriate here. No matter how thorough the evaluator is in constructing questions, some questions will be overlooked, or they will become evident when reviewing the data. This phenomenon is a fairly common one even among experienced evaluators and should not be a cause for undue concern. The data collected from evaluation will always provide different perspectives on issues and a new set of questions to ask.

Demographic data should be included in the evaluation form. The kind of information the evaluator wants about the people answering the questions should be limited to the way the information is going to be used in analysis. For example, if the evaluator wants to know how people with more schooling answered questions compared to those with less schooling, then respondents need to be asked how much schooling they have had. If a comparison is being made between how older and younger people responded, then the ages of those answering the questions are needed. Thinking about how the results will be reported and used is the best way to determine which demographic data to collect.

Coverage of the subject is important. The information needed should be gathered and no more. It is tempting to ask a few more interesting questions than are really needed. After all, the construction of items, printing, and mailing cost money and so why not collect as much data as possible? This temptation should be resisted. It will dilute the real reason for asking the questions, it will compromise face validity, and it will confuse the person answering the questions.

The design of the evaluation is important. Design refers to more than how the questionnaire is laid out or how the questions appear. It has to do with when people will be surveyed, interviewed, or both. It has to do with who will be interviewed or surveyed and how they will be chosen. It has to do with what kinds of questions the evaluation will answer. By questions I don't mean the ones on a survey or in an interview. Questions refer to the global ones, such as "Does this program make any difference?" or "How do trainers feel about this policy?"

Design involves the scope and timing of evaluation activities. It is similar to research design activities, but instead of wishing for laboratory conditions evaluators embrace the "field" as an actual situation and one that can be understood. Designs are meant to show what conditions pertain and what effects they may have.

The context of the evaluation dictates its design. For example, we were recently asked to evaluate the beginnings of a quality circle program. The employees were having a difficult time initiating the program. In reality, there was not a program to evaluate. This is not an uncommon problem. What should the evaluation look like? One of the assumptions I have as an evaluator is that I will be helpful to the people who hire me. In this case, our team of evaluators decided that the best service we could be to this group was to hold up a mirror for the group and let them see themselves as they really were. We approached the matter through interviews of the employees and with a survey of their clients. With this information the group could move forward in installing the program and in understanding where they as a group and their clients stood on issues about quality circles.

As well as design, the actual skills of capturing the data are important to an evaluation. Interviewing skills are important and should be briefly discussed here because no matter how well a protocol (interview guide) is constructed, unless the interviewer has some skills the information will be suspect. Lack of interviewing skills can cancel out all of the good work in designing the evaluation and constructing the instruments. An inept interviewer can invalidate an evaluation.

What are the skills of a good interviewer? First, an interviewer must be a good listener. A good listener in this sense is not one who idly sits and lets the other person talk. Rather, it is one who actively listens and actually draws the speaker out. This is done by demonstrating interest in what the interviewee is saying. Interest is shown by acknowledging what has been said either by repeating what was heard (this is actually a good way to validate conclusions from an interview) or by asking questions about what has been said. I often use myself as a "foil" in the sense that I say something like, "Now let me see if I understand what you have said." It allows me to stay in control of the conversation. Even though this statement does not direct the discussion, it keeps me involved and ready to control it if the person should wander too far from the focus of the interview. I take notes during an interview, even though the tape recorder does a much better job than I could ever do. (I cannot record the voice inflections or exact words.) My notes are notes to me about what I should be asking next. They are to jog my memory and to see if I have asked questions that have been raised during the interview. I think this also demonstrates interest on my part about what is being said.

Second, probes are used by good interviewers. These probes

can either focus ("Tell me more about. . . . ") or widen the area of discussion ("Are there any related factors to this situation?"). Probes are expressions of wanting to find more out about the subject and are also elements of control in the discussion. Control of the discussion is important. An interview is a chance for the interviewee to explain what he or she knows about the subject. It is a chance to learn.

Third, a good interviewer says very little during an interview. If the interviewer is speaking more than 5% of the time, it is not an interview; it is something else.

Fourth, good interviewers do not lead their subjects. They provide the interviewee no clues about personal views or opinions. The best way to do this is to use the first three elements listed above.

Recording information during an interview is different from recording information on a questionnaire. A debate used to exist about the advisability of tape recording versus note taking during an interview. The widespread use of hand-held tape recorders has minimized that debate a great deal. Research has also demonstrated that the quality of information is no different when information is tape recorded versus when it is written. Research has also shown that tape recording has the most effect on the person doing the interview. For some reason, interviewers continually check the tape recorder to see if it is working, thus detracting from the interview. The quality of taped interviews are much better than handwritten notes where lapses or ambiguous notations are present.

After taping hundreds of interviews, I have had only one failure, and it was recoverable. After interviewing a school superintendent, I listened to the interview and found the tape faded about 30 minutes into the hour-long interview. A professional recording company looked for it through their various filters but could not find the missing conversation. Reinterviewing became the only solution. I made a compressed transcript of the first part of our interview and then called the superintendent and explained my problem. He and I reviewed the recorded part of the interview and then continued with another interview from that point.

ANALYZING THE DATA

Data analysis is perhaps one of the most troublesome parts of evaluation for many people, probably because it is hard to understand the complex world of statistics and how statistics can be used. In this section three simple statistical approaches or tools used most often by evaluators are described: distributions, means, and standard deviations. Readers with statistical needs that go beyond these tools should consult a statistician. Other sources of help can be found in introductory research texts such as Frankel and Wallen (1990), Leedy (1989), and Gay (1991). These kinds of books do not go into depth but provide an understanding of what is available to the interested person.

The most overlooked but basic tool is the frequency distribution. It is a table of all of the response values laid out from the highest to the lowest. Table 5.1 contains the results of a recent survey in a frequency distribution. A reader can quickly determine how many people fall into which age group and what percent of the total they represent.

Table 5.1 Survey results in a frequency distribution

Age value label	Value	Frequency	Percent	Valid percent	Cum percent
21–30	1	2	5.9	5.9	5.9
31–40	2	8	23.5	23.5	29.4
41–50	3	11	32.4	32.4	61.8
51–60	4	7	20.6	20.6	82.4
61–70	5	5	14.7	14.7	97.1
71 and over	6	1	2.9	2.9	100.0
Total		34	100.0	100.0	

Using data from a frequency distribution, a histogram is easily constructed. Histograms are graphs that provide a visual representation of the numbers from a distribution. Some people

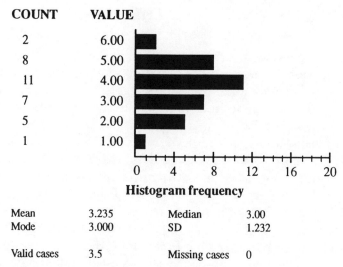

COUNT	VALUE
2	6.00
8	5.00
11	4.00
7	3.00
5	2.00
1	1.00

Histogram frequency

Mean	3.235	Median	3.00
Mode	3.000	SD	1.232
Valid cases	3.5	Missing cases	0

Figure 5.3   Survey results in a histogram

cannot relate to numbers in a table, but they can easily relate to the picture of the numbers that graphs provide.

The next statistical tool that is easily calculated is the mean or average. Actually the mean, median, and mode are all averages, but the mean is technically called the arithmetic average because it is calculated by using every score in the distribution. To calculate the mean, simply add all of the scores and then divide that sum by the number of scores; that result is the mean. The mean from the table above is 3.23. The mean gives a measure of how the scores tended to the middle of the distribution. However, it does not supply a measure of how widely spread the scores are. Look at Figure 5.3 and compare it to Figure 5.4. Notice that the means are very similar, the scores spread further apart in Figure 5.3. These are two different patterns of response.

A third tool, the standard deviation (SD), completes the picture of the scores. Just as the mean is considered a measure or index of how scores tend to clump together, the SD measures how the scores tend to spread apart. This is a valuable notion

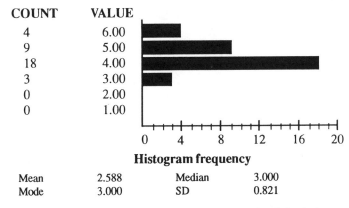

COUNT	VALUE
4	6.00
9	5.00
18	4.00
3	3.00
0	2.00
0	1.00

Histogram frequency

Mean	2.588	Median	3.000
Mode	3.000	SD	0.821

Figure 5.4   Survey results with a smaller standard deviation

because the same mean could be calculated on two related items, but there could be a wider division of opinion on one than another, similar to Figures 5.3 and 5.4.

To calculate the SD, first create a frequency distribution (list every score in a column). Second, calculate the mean. Third, subtract the mean from every score and enter that result in a second column. Fourth, square each entry in this column and then enter the result in a third column. Fifth, add this column. Sixth, divide this result by the number of scores. Seventh, take the square root. The result is the standard deviation. Notice that the standard deviation includes how far each score is from the mean. It is a measure of the spread of the scores.

Table 5.2 demonstrates how the standard deviation is calculated. Using the data from Table 5.2, the sum of the scores minus the mean (the total of the third column) is divided by 11 (the number of scores) and the answer is 2.21. Next, the square root of 2.21 is taken (because we squared the score minus the mean and are now returning it to the unsquared state). The answer is 1.48, the standard deviation for this set of scores.

Understanding these tools can help an evaluator communicate findings from an evaluation as well as understand find-

Table 5.2   Calculation of a standard deviation

Scores	Score minus the mean	Score minus the mean squared
4	.2	.4
5	1.2	1.44
6	2.2	4.84
6	2.2	4.84
2	-1.8	3.24
3	- .8	.64
2	-1.8	3.24
3	- .8	.64
2	-1.8	3.24
4	.2	.4
5	1.2	1.44

Sum = 42   Sum = 24.36

Mean = 3.8

ings from other studies. These tools are meant to communicate concepts such as how scores group together or spread apart.

Qualitative are another kind of data evaluators often report to stakeholders. These data are not meant to show how widespread some idea or feeling is; rather, they attempt to show how deep, simple, or complex feelings or situations are. Instead of presenting information about a group of people, qualitative data tell about a problem. They help the user understand individual perspectives on an issue. Therefore, such information should be presented differently. Qualitative data can be presented as numbers (there is nothing wrong with numbers representing qualities). Qualitative data should be presented as qualities; therefore, they should be presented in mostly a narrative mode.

Qualitative researchers do use numbers to show the extend of some problem or opinion. They often use means, standard deviations, and other statistical tools. However, their main interest is not in showing that some group of people are representative of the rest of the group. Their interest is in describing the problem. Most competent researchers and evaluators use both approaches to complement one another. A thorough evaluation will help stakeholders understand both a feeling or a problem and how widespread it is. Once data are collected in a narrative manner, they undergo a two-stage analysis. The first is a production of a compressed transcript of the interviews. Compressed transcripts differ from fully typed transcripts in that every word is not transcribed. The full text of the interview is on tape and there is little need to spend time typing it out if a compressed transcript is used. Compressed transcripts are translations in as few words as possible. When important quotes are located, these are typed fully. Compressed transcripts are also indexed by using the tape counter found on many recorders. If an evaluator wants to refer to a specific part of the interview, it is relatively easy to locate.

The second stage of the analysis involves producing an evaluation analysis matrix, which will be described in detail in Chapter 7.

FORMING CONCLUSIONS

Conclusions are difficult things to come to. Often an evaluator will wonder if he or she has enough information to form sound conclusions. I have been part of an evaluation where the senior evaluator was willing to make conclusions after a second meeting with some stakeholders and before data were collected. The data we collect often support our initial hunches or guesses. It is not an improper strategy to set up conclusions initially. However, it is incorrect to hold to those conclusions when the data do not support them. It is also inappropriate not to challenge them.

Some evaluators use these preformed conclusions as working hypotheses in that they try to disprove them. When an hypothesis is disproved, then we should have alternative hypotheses or guesses to explain a problem or an opinion.

One of the most useful tools in forming conclusions are

demographic data. These refer to the description of the people involved in a survey or interviews. In survey information, a breakdown of how people feel by level of education, kind of employee, length of service, or other personal information that has been gathered can be presented. The time to consider how the information should be broken down is before the evaluation is done. For example, recently I did an evaluation of a number of distance education courses. We decided before we did the evaluation that we wanted to know several things from the evaluation. Among them were information about the colleges involved, the level of the courses taught, the location of the course (where the receiving sites were located), and the size of the course. It was essential that this information be gathered at the same time as individual student opinions about the courses were gathered.

Deciding how the information is to be analyzed in advance of data collection will save an evaluator hours of detail work. It will save a sponsor of evaluation thousands of dollars.

When the data are analyzed, trends and groupings are easily found. These trends point to conclusions. This is where the statement "let the data speak for themselves" comes from. Such a statement is debated by some who feel that numbers or data never speak for themselves, but it is the evaluator who does the speaking. I tend to agree with this kind of thinking. However, some trends and groupings fairly call out to be recognized. It is these kinds of trends and groupings that help evaluators form conclusions.

Some people feel they must have statistically significant findings before trends are reported. Remember, a trend is a trend even if the findings are not significant statistically. A concept called *practical significance* should be emphasized here. Sometimes statistical significance can be obtained and not mean much at all. For example, we performed a study and found a correlation or a relationship between two groups of .06 to be significant statistically. This means only that an extremely weak relationship existed and that the study groups were different. The coefficient of .06 had no practical value. Evaluators need to examine just what they are studying and what kinds of findings would be significant. Most of the findings do not need statistical significance to be important, only to be representative of a population. Many evaluations are surveys of the entire population; significance has no relevance for these kinds of evaluations.

MAKING RECOMMENDATIONS

Recommendations are often ignored or avoided by evaluators. Reasons for this include mistaken ideas of what evaluation is about, the organizational role of an evaluator, and reluctance of individuals to make recommendations that may be somewhat controversial. Each of these reasons are next considered to show how they can be overcome or compensated for.

Mistaken Roles for Evaluation

Many people think that evaluation is only for making judgments about the value of a project, person, or organization. This idea likely comes from insisting that the collection of data is not enough to be called evaluation and that some act of "valuing" has to be engaged in before the full notion of e"valu"ation is realized. Today, the notion of valuing is a fairly standard practice with some exceptions being found among those who do not understand evaluation or who are new to the field.

What is not well understood is that evaluation should be a helpful undertaking, that the results should mean something to stakeholders. I remember doing an image evaluation for an organization. I offered the results and some recommendations that were never, to my knowledge, implemented. Perhaps the recommendations were incorrect or wrongheaded, but I doubt it because I worked with the organization head and other employees to make certain recommendations were feasible and acceptable to the unit. I also offered to help the organization implement the recommendations after the head requested I do so. It must be stressed that implementing recommendations is something different from evaluation, although they are closely related. Whenever recommendations are implemented, evaluators engage in organization development, which is a different task from evaluation. Evaluators work at the edges of organization development and should be prepared to move into the area with little or no reservation, but they should move in a competent way.

Organizational Role of an Evaluator

As discussed above, evaluation works at the edges of organization development. The edges are supplying information to decision makers. The debate about whether an internal or external evaluator should be used has many dimensions, and this is one of them. Influencing organizational change is a role for an internal evaluator. This person knows who makes what kinds of decisions and how people make those decisions. He or she understands the kind of information and the proper format for the information needed to influence those decisions makers. In a few words, an internal evaluator is more powerful in changing an organization than is an external evaluator.

Some people will contend, and correctly so, that there are occasions where an external evaluator will have a more pronounced impact than will an internal one. I agree, and when I, as an internal, know that is the case, I will contract with an outside evaluator. It cannot be the other way around. An external cannot contract with an internal. However, there is a way in which an external can use internal evaluators. We recently investigated a program in a community college to see what the administration, faculty, and students thought about it. There was controversy about the program, so we proceeded with some care. We used an administrator as "part" of the evaluation. This person was not the official contact for the contract.

However, he was an important access to the level of decision makers we need to interact with. Establishing the contact was accomplished by asking the person for his opinions about the program and then explaining what we as evaluators were trying to do. Cooperation was informal and effective in this manner.

An internal evaluator has the chance to influence his or her organization on a continual and constant basis. In my organization I am not in the decision-making path, but I influence it in a number of ways. The first way has been alluded to: the kinds of reports and information I provide and the way in which they are provided. The second way is that I "feed forward" as opposed to feedback information. I let the decision makers know what is coming and enlist their help in deciding the best way to present the information. With this approach they use the information as theirs, they will more likely use it for making important decisions, and I will more likely influence the decisions made. The third way I influence the decision makers is to understand their goals and directions. Such an understanding enables me to be sensitive to what they need and to how information will likely be needed. These elements help internal evaluators exert more influence than external evaluators can ever think of having. Internals should remember that they will be in an organization long after the external has gone.

Reluctance of Evaluators to Make Controversial Recommendations

Some recommendations are controversial because they may favor one group or another; they may provide uncomfortable messages for a stakeholder; or they may involve moving a person, group, or organization out of their comfort zone. These situations can be largely avoided by the feed forward principle discussed earlier. Involvement of the stakeholders from the initial design of an evaluation, with increasing participation of stakeholders as an evaluation nears its conclusion, is an important aspect.

SUMMARY

This chapter explored standards, sources of evidence, instrument construction, and interviewing skills as ways to collect and analyze data. It also discussed ways in which data should be recorded. A very brief discussion of some common statistical tools was included as well. Forming conclusions and making recommendations as part of evaluation was discussed. The importance of demographic data in this effort was pointed out.

CHAPTER 6

Evaluating Organizations

Organizations can be evaluated just as people and programs can be appraised. It is a more complex job to do so, and there is no one who is going to make a recommendation about a pay raise or promotion for an organization. However, there are people who have a stake in how an organization is doing and how it is performing. These people need recommendations and a have a desire for an organization to do well in the future.

Obvious stakeholders include owners of organizations. Public organizations are supported by tax dollars contributed by the public, the ultimate stakeholder. Each year the public elects individuals to represent them at local, state, and national levels. They become the elected stakeholders to whom public organizations are accountable.

Other stakeholders include customers of an organization. They are voluntary customers in the private sector and involuntary customers in the public sector. In the private sectors, clients can leave and find services elsewhere. This is not so in the public sector; clients have to get services from the public agency or go without. Evaluation of the organization becomes a tool for making certain the client is being served.

Additional stakeholders include the employees of the organization. Their interest is in making sure the organization is healthy and will continue to provide a good place to work. Additionally, they may have some vision of where the organization should be going and evaluations may supply a way to measure or otherwise locate that direction.

Yet another group of stakeholders includes the organization's managers. Managers have interests in the organization as a place in which to work, to accomplish professional goals, and to express individual value to society. Any evaluation that is conducted with these motivations as backdrops will likely be different from evaluations with other motivations. Some managers may have solely a profit orientation, while others may have a social orientation. These orientations influence the kinds of evaluations conducted and areas emphasized. The following are several broad areas for evaluation in organizations: morale, organizational structure, administration/management, effectiveness, and planning. These areas are all important organization structures or processes. Each one will be considered in this chapter.

MORALE

Morale is one area for measuring how well an organization is doing and what kind of place it is to work. It is the contextual health of an agency. An organization with low morale may just limp along never becoming an excellent organization. Morale refers to three specific things. The first thing is how well employees like working for a particular organization. Do they like their co-workers? Do they like working for their supervisor? Do they feel valued? Would they rather be off work or at work? All of these items can be measured with instruments or through interviews. A company could even plot days absent from work as a index of morale.

The second part of morale is how well employees like the kind of work they are doing. Is their work challenging? Is it boring? Can they use their individual judgment in getting the work done?

The third part of morale is how well employees like working for the management team. Are they truly managers? Do they listen to employee ideas? Do managers have the interests of the individual worker in mind? Interviews offer much to an evaluation in terms of morale.

People are willing to share their impressions of how well an organization is doing. I was once conducting a focus group interview with employees of a community college, and they quickly let me know how they felt about a specific person. Their quickness to be candid was amazing to me. People are willing to share their feelings and observations when trust is established.

CHANGING ORGANIZATIONAL STRUCTURE

Once problems in an organization have been documented and demonstrated either through survey methods, interviews, or critical incidents (Witken, 1984), the time for action is at hand. When the problems deal with an ineffective and inefficient structure, then it must be changed in some manner. Changes to an organizational structure take various forms: deletions, additions, and modifications. Any of these changes is traumatic in nature. What manager or employee wants to see some or all of his or her division eliminated from a company? What manager or employee willingly gives up some or all of his or her division to a colleague? Most managers welcome additions to their areas of responsibility; however, additions affect others. The employees in a division may resent the new addition or otherwise not concur with the actions taken. Changing organization structure is a delicate but important matter. Many people have much invested in such an endeavor.

These potential problems can be lessened somewhat by an open style of organizational change. This style of openness means that affected divisions are somehow involved in the decision-making process. The process of how organizational change comes about and how widely that process might be shared within a company will now be examined. First, a narrow approach is considered.

After a problem is well understood (which is a role for evaluation), different scenarios are developed by a team of planners. This team may be officially appointed by company executives or it may be an ad hoc team that naturally has a stake in the changes. The scenarios are presented in formal or informal ways and their pros and cons debated, usually by a narrow and restricted group of people. The favored plan is forwarded to top management who makes the final decision. Because the plan is not widely shared and is often done in secret, employees are sometimes shocked to hear the final decision.

If the scenario is changed a bit, as many people as possible can be involved in the process. This is a time for imaginative thinking. By casting the net as widely as possible (not as practical), more brain power is harnessed and put to work on the problem.

The act of evaluation plays an important role at this point in time. Top management will want to know the effects of the process (not the change, as that will come later) on the rest of the organization. Spot checks regarding morale should be taken with appropriate samples while the process of change is taking place. A rapid evaluation method should be employed. Rapid refers to quickly administered, gathered, analyzed, and reported. Before the change process begins, the evaluation function should be in place with baseline information available. Some notice should be given to those people responsible for evaluation. Samples can be drawn, instruments can be developed, and analysis plans can be devised before any questionnaire is administered. If evaluators have standing appointments with top management to report results, they will have them ready.

As the structure is changed, management can have weekly (or more often) reports on the effects of the process. These reports can assist management in knowing what information is needed to help the organization respond to the needs of the employees.

An example can be given of what is meant by a rapid response on the part of the evaluation function. Suppose that in an organization of 1,000 workers, a division of 200 people was going to be eliminated over a 6-month period. Employee attitudes would be sampled in two places: within the divisions that remain and within the division that is being eliminated. The reason is that many rumors may likely start with the division scheduled for elimination. The organization would be surveyed at prespecified times, with the understanding that some adjustment may be needed depending on the situation.

The timing of the surveys would be coordinated with announcements coming from management. Management usually has reasons for making announcements, so it is important for the evaluator to know what those reasons are so that he or she might design data gathering to see if the objectives set by management have been met, and if so, to what degree they are being met. Timing does not have to be at regular intervals; it might well vary over the 6-month period. It is important to gather data more often at the beginning and at the end than it is at the middle of a time period. Whenever organizations take drastic action, the beginning is a time of confusion and rumors. The end is usually predictive of attitudes that might remain within the company.

Gathering data from two areas was mentioned: from the affected division and from the rest of the organization. This is done to trace any effects from the affected part of the organization to the rest of the organization. Results can inform managers if they should place their efforts in the division that is affected, in the rest of the organization, or both.

This example of using evaluation techniques and skills as a monitoring device is a formative type of evaluation intended to serve the objectives of management and to help plan future steps. Such a plan should use small samples in order to avoid high costs and to avoid disturbing too many people. A systematic approach such as the one described above will give more accurate readings than will exit interviews, which are often not handled in a systematic manner.

CHANGING ORGANIZATION ADMINISTRATION

Sometimes organizational problems lie not with structure, but with management. When this is the case, the evaluator finds himself or herself in a difficult position. The news the evaluator carries may be distasteful to management and may be a hard pill to swallow. Management may not be willing to hear the message or to change behaviors. When such is the case, the evaluator plays an informal but important leadership role. Credibility becomes important and trust is essential. If these two elements have been established in other settings and at other times through evaluation studies, the evaluator will find his or her task easier. This is especially true of internal evaluators (those employed by an organization on a full-time basis).

One tactic for helping managers (and almost anyone else) see problems is to present the data and ask them for assistance in interpretation. It may be difficult for the management group to admit they are the basis of a problem, but if they come to that conclusion themselves, then the evaluator's job is much easier because they "own" the problem.

If this tactic is used, it is essential for the evaluator to have possible explanations and corrective actions in mind. After all, no one else in an organization has the total picture of the problem and has studied it as much as has the evaluator. The nature of the problem and its effects often suggest possible ways to remedy the situation.

Once I worked in a large organization that had a group of top managers located at headquarters and a second group of line mangers spread over a large geographical area. We did a morale study for the organization and found that the second-line managers were trusted and respected. At the same time, there was not much trust and respect for the top managers. Certainly the location of top management contributed to the problem. Privately, I presented the information to the CEO and asked for his assessment, which turned out to be my assessment. He then asked that I share it with the other top managers and then with the second-line managers. At subsequent meetings the CEO presented the data and made suggestions for correction. My role was only to offer the information and support his observations. The corrective action came from the top and was accepted much better than if I had made the presentations and conclusions.

But what if the CEO had not been open and could not see the obvious? What if he had an ostrich attitude? In that event I was prepared to offer alternative conclusions and a set of suggestions. Evaluation activities, especially in this arena of operation, have to be a negotiated effort. Suggestions and recommendations take the place of solid conclusions and remedies.

ORGANIZATIONAL FUNCTIONS

Organizational functions refer to the work an organization does. It is described in terms of effectiveness, and effectiveness refers to doing things well. It is here that evaluation plays a continual role whether in an informal or formal sense. It refers to impact. Effectiveness for an organization is a measure of the following: Does it communicate well, set goals that are shared, have cooperation as the norm, have management that functions as a team, have employees that have regard for one another, use its resources, and have a feedback mechanism in place? Each one of these areas can be measured by various items on a questionnaire or through interviews with employees and management.

EVALUATING FOR EFFICIENCY

All organizations attempt to be efficient; they want to accomplish goals with the least amount of effort and expenditures of resources. Evaluation plays a role in this regard and the cost/benefit model of evaluation becomes important. In this kind of evaluation the evaluator does not study as much as he or she measures. The cost/benefit model assumes there are units of input and output available for measurement. Each unit of input is traceable to a unit of output. Divisions can trace efforts and contributions to the total value of the finished article.

The cost/benefit model has been summarized by Brinkerhoff (1987). He offers these six steps: (1) Identify decision makers and their values; (2) Identify possible program alternatives; (3) Identify costs; (4) Identify benefits; (5) Convert benefits into comparable data with costs; and (6) Interpret the effects. Steps

1, 2, and 6 are not unique to cost/benefit analysis; they are important steps in other evaluation models. Steps 3, 4, and 5 constitute the heart of cost/benefit analysis and provide its unique flavor.

While applying these steps may seem fairly straightforward, some words of caution about applying cost/benefit analysis are appropriate here. Sometimes an organization does not lend itself well to such analysis. For example, schools have a very difficult time in measuring its output in terms of dollars. They also have an extremely difficult time determining which factors contributed how much to what outcomes. Any educational agency has similar kinds of difficulty.

A number of years ago it was fashionable to compare public organizations to "domesticated" organizations and private organizations to "wild" organizations. The intent was to provide a prospective that public agencies do not have to compete for clients or resources. This has changed substantially in that public agencies are competing for clients and operating in wild environments. However, the terms *wild* and *domesticated* are useful if they are removed from the organization and used to describe organizations' environments. Some organizations operate in a domestic environment where future behavior is more easily predicted than in a wild environment. Today, it seems as though wild environments are more prevalent for public and private organizations than they have been in the past. Prediction is no longer as easy as it once was for public organizations. Such environments do not lend themselves readily to cost/benefit analysis, especially in organizations that are basically people-processing or people-changing organizations.

Whenever people are objects to be affected by an organization such as a school, a prison, or a training department, the measurement in a cost/benefit sense becomes difficult. This is compounded when training or education involves attitude changes or other less readily measured outcomes.

Evaluators should not take this difficulty personally. They share with others in the imprecision. When evaluators or trainers are given a task to evaluate in the "soft skills" area, they should request that baseline data be provided so they can understand what kinds of gains are made because of training. If baseline data do not exist, then they may be a little more relaxed realizing that it is not their task alone to verify the effectiveness of training.

Cost/benefit analysis assumes that dollar amounts can be fixed to costs and benefits. Sometimes this fixing of dollars is rather subjective and incomplete. For example, suppose evaluators are asked to evaluate a companywide safety program. The costs for such training are instructional costs, logistics, heat, and missed production time (hence dollars), but the benefits may not be so easily identified. The difference between the monthly absence rate before and after the training can be calculated in a straightforward manner. However, the value of disabilities and lives saved is a different matter; this is much more difficult to determine because such values have more than a dollar equivalent.

What about a training session in communications skills, arbitration, or other equally soft areas? The costs are always more easily fixed than the benefits. There may be some indirect (and hence less defendable) measures like employee turnover.

One important part of cost/benefit analysis is agreement on how benefits will be measured and valued. Once this is accomplished, the participants in the program must understand what will be measured because the measures may change the nature of a program. For example, if instructors knew that the results of their safety training program were going to be measured in terms of absentee days, they might give it a different "twist" than if disabilities were going to be measured.

Recently, my university directed all of its employees to attend a workshop on sexual harassment in the workplace. As I sat through the session, I wondered how cost/benefit might be applied. The workshop may have very well increased the number of complaints to the Equal Employment Opportunity office. A cost/benefit analysis would have produced a negative result. However, when measured on other factors, it may have resulted in huge savings for the university. Costly court cases may have been avoided. Suffering by employees (the victims) may have been reduced. But how can these things be valued? The benefit side of the analysis is not easily measured.

STRATEGIC PLANNING AND EVALUATING

Strategic planning and evaluation are often treated as separate concepts and endeavors. A union of these two concepts is needed. Evaluation efforts are often divided into two grand divisions: formative and summative. Summative evaluations are those efforts that provide a sum total of the program or change effects. It is a pronouncement at the end of an activity about the results of that activity. It is a response to accountability.

On the other hand, formative evaluation is an activity meant to supply information that will guide efforts to product a better end result. It supplies corrective information to our efforts in programs or other change-producing activities.

Strategic planning is a set of activities meant to help an organization change to meet some designated outcome or goal. The achievement of the goal cannot be realized without some midcourse corrections. It is much like the Apollo missions discussed earlier. The success of these missions depended on vital information to decision makers about the next movement of the space vehicle. This, in a sense, is all formative information.

The same principle is true for strategic plans. Strategic plans are visions of where an organization wants to go. To achieve this movement, some changes in what is done may be needed. An organization may have to let go of some old products or processes. To move into these new areas, milestones are set and used as markers to guide the proper movement toward a goal. Information given to managers about how well or completely milestones have been achieved is supplying midcourse evaluation data to individuals who are making decisions about the strategic plan.

Strategic plans are visions of the future that are commonly shared among the members of an organization. There are many approaches for doing strategic planning. While these approaches are not the subject of this text, it is important to understand evaluation's relationship to strategic plans.

Evaluation and strategic planning go hand in hand in making an organization a better thing. Strategic planning and its execution rely on sound information, providing a role for evaluation.

I was once involved in strategic planning for a large organization. The chair of the strategic planning committee had a vision of what the end results should be; however, those results were never shared with the committee. The chair was a powerful personality and he never asked the committee for its views on issues and opportunities. Members of the committee tried to explain, but we were more or less filibustered. He never formally or informally surveyed the committee. He did hold open hearings for the organization's employees to discuss plans, but he ignored data that didn't match his ideas. Now, years later his strategic plan is not in place.

SUMMARY

Evaluating organizations takes different forms as its objectives differ. The evaluation function is a monitoring device for innovation or other changes to an organization. Morale, structure, administration, and functions are all possible areas for evaluation in an organizational context. Involvement of the stakeholders, management, and clients are important to achieve the best possible results from an evaluation activity. The evaluator, especially an internal evaluator, may find his or her position to be somewhat difficult at times, but the involvement of others in the process of design, data collection, and especially interpretation, reporting, and conclusion making can help the results be used and accepted.

CHAPTER 7

Strategies for Evaluating Organizations

This chapter provides steps an evaluator or manager can follow in making determinations about organizations. The focus of evaluation changes here from the focus in chapter 3 to include nonliving entities such as schools, businesses, churches, museums, and the like. While it was noted that organizations are nonliving things, a persuasive argument can be made that they are in reality similar to living things. For example, organizations go through growth or developmental stages just like people. There are young organizations that behave in childish ways, there are aggressive organizations, there are old organizations, and there is such a thing as organizational memory. Organizations do get old and some of them die. Some of them get hardening of the arteries. They have surgeries (cutbacks), some cosmetic (new public relations campaigns) and some radical (restructuring).

Therefore, evaluating organizations may well involve some of the principles used in evaluating people. Certainly some of the same indicators can be used. The elements of evaluating organizations are similar to those described in Chapter 3. Differences are in the way the elements are carried out and in their focus. Each element is described in this chapter in some detail in terms of evaluating organizations.

CHOOSING THE INDICATORS

The statement, "The indicators used to evaluate an organization depend. . . . " should be a somewhat familiar theme to those who have read chapters 1 through 6. Careful selection of indicators is based on a clear understanding of what the objectives of the evaluation are. The first step in selecting indicators is to define the evaluation objectives. This step involves talking with mangers, CEOs, and employees who will be affected by or who are requesting the evaluation. Whether a person is an internal or an external evaluator, he or she should get input from various stakeholders as to what is to be evaluated. Once an evaluator has an understanding about what is wanted, he or she can then move to asking this same group of people what they would consider as evidence for evaluation findings. Not all people should have equal weight in determining indicators. Some people have a better perspective on potential indicators and should be listened to more than others.

If an evaluator is tuned in to the fact that evaluations are political, as discussed in chapter 1, it will not be a surprise when opposition is expressed to the results or to the fact that an evaluation is even taking place. Indicators are one place that an evaluation's political impacts can be lessened through negotiation. Negotiation does not mean that potentially embarrassing indicators are watered down or eliminated. Negotiating means that the parties involved have a chance to make their concerns known to the evaluator.

For example, suppose an evaluator has been asked to evaluate a teamwork training program for managers. This sounds like a fairly apolitical situation until it is discovered that the CEO or president wants the evaluation to take place and that the head of training is afraid of the potential results. This is her flagship training program and she does not want to put it at risk. In these kinds of situations some programs will likely be at risk and the evaluator, if not circumspect, will not have the support of the head of training. It is important that the CEO and head of training both comment on the indicators. In this example the evaluator could enlist the aid of the head of training to help in selecting the indicators and then get the agreement of the CEO. The evaluator's role might be to suggest and comment on those that are selected. However, the evaluator would be misinformed if the experience of both people were not employed in establishing and commenting on the indicators.

Where does one find indicators? Are they out there, just waiting to be used? One place to find them is the goals of the organization or the objectives of a program. These are indispensable in looking for indicators. If a program is intended to reduce the amount of rejections from a manufacturing process, then the evaluator will look for reduced rejections as an indicator of success. If the program is intended to increase the amount of understanding of principles of good management, then the evaluator will look to increased understanding of management principles. Indicators are buried in the objectives of programs.

Sometimes objectives are rather foggy and hard to understand. If this is the case, the evaluator engages in defogging operations. This can be done by asking several short, but important questions. Some of them are: "How do I know if the program has had effects on participants?" "How do I know if this is an excellent organization?" "What should it be like to make me think it is excellent?" These questions are really questions of evidence. Evidence is what the stakeholders are willing to accept as proof that a program or organization meets expectations.

Indicators have to be measurable or they will not serve the needed purposes. Sometimes they are suggested with little or no thought about their measurability. The following steps for making an indicator measurable are based on Mager's (1972) work on making instructional objectives measurable.

Step 1. Write the indicator down. Don't be concerned with whether or not it is measurable. The important thing is to capture what it should mean. Some indicators that are not readily measurable include a positive atmosphere, dynamic leadership, and a creative organization.

Step 2. List some items that would count as evidence an indicator is present. For example, use "a positive atmosphere" as an indicator. What items should be accepted as evidence? The following indicators are possibilities.

- The employees smile.
- The employees speak positively of self and others.
- The employees take responsibility for tasks.
- Opinions are expressed freely.
- Employees and supervisors have a good attitude.
- Employees and management cooperate.
- Individuals maintain eye-to-eye contact.
- People volunteer for assignments.
- The absentee rate is lower than average.

Step 3. Sort the items into concrete (observable or measurable) or abstract evidence. Note that all indicators on the list above are concrete except for the fifth one. A good attitude is abstract, so it will be set aside for the time being.

Step 4. Write coherent statements about what is meant by each of the items classified as concrete listed in step 2 above. The following are examples of statements related to the items.

- Employees in a company with a positive atmosphere will smile more often than those in a company with a negative or neutral atmosphere.
- In a unit or division where a positive atmosphere exists, employees will speak in positive terms about fellow members or others.
- Employees in a company with a positive atmosphere will accept responsibility for their actions.
- Employees in a company with a positive atmosphere will verbally express their opinions.

Step 5. Review what has been written and ask, Do these statements provide evidence for the indicator we began with? If the answer is yes, these statements can be used as evaluation indicators. If the answer is no, the process should be repeated.

What about the one abstraction that was set aside in step 3? It becomes the subject of the five-step process just explained.

To increase the validity of this exercise, a colleague should be asked to make judgments about the list that was developed. Once the indicators are in place, the process of setting standards can begin.

SETTING THE STANDARDS

Standards refer to how much of an indicator is needed in order to judge whether an organization is at some level of excellence. What level of an indicator is acceptable in order to show a group is doing OK or excellent? One way of doing this is to determine how much it costs to collect the data. Another way is to determine what minimal level an organization can tolerate. Still another way is to determine how much of an indicator the organization needs to be effective or excellent. An example can make these rather vague statements realistic.

Suppose an evaluator has been asked to determine the level of positive atmosphere in a unit within a large organization. The evaluator can refer to the process outlined above that specifys the evidence that will be accepted as indicators of a positive atmosphere. With an unlimited budget, all of the items outlined could be measured. But what if the evaluator was given a few hundred dollars and was asked to provide a reading? Then the process would be to select the best indicator within the budget given. It might be that interviewing or surveying what fellow employees think of one another is the only action affordable. Therefore, the standards will be set according to what the budget is likely to produce. It makes no sense to set standards in such a way that the indicators are beyond measurement. The budget has limited what can be dealt with.

What an organization is willing to tolerate is another way of setting the standards. This sets the minimum levels needed for an organization to function. This situation is best exemplified by organizational effectiveness and efficiency. What is the minimum level of production needed to remain in business? What is the minimum level of absenteeism that can be tolerated by an organization? This approach to setting the standards for indicators is a minimum criterion approach. What can an organization tolerate and still succeed?

The last approach to setting standards is to determine what levels need to be achieved for excellence. It is just the opposite from the minimum criterion approach. Other similar organizations may well be studied for information in setting levels. This is much like a comparative needs analysis. If an organization wants to be as excellent as the Marriott Corporation in terms of service, then it should look at how Marriott's service is rewarded and how employees are trained. Results of these comparisons will help those involved set standards. Because of their far reaching implications, decision makers should be involved in setting these standards.

Standards in judging an organization are different from standards in judging individuals. When evaluating people was considered, a criterion-referenced standard (not acceptable, below expectations, meets expectations, exceeds expectations, and extraordinary) was used. Such standards are not appropriate for an organization. What is appropriate is a comparison to baseline data. For example, the number of sick days used by all employees can be measured and then compared after some type of intervention takes place. A morale survey taken at one point in time and compared to results from another point in time will show differences.

SELECTING THE SOURCES

Sources for information about an organization should include those records that tell (or individuals who know) something about the selected indicators. Evaluators often make the mistake of assuming people have more information than they really do. Consider this question: "In your opinion, does the warehouse meet the demands of shippers' schedules with the current number of employees?" This is a perfectly sound question. The problem comes when the question is asked of people who know very little of the warehouse, who do not know how many employees work in the warehouse, and who do not know the shippers' schedules. Often a mistake is made in assuming too much knowledge from sources. Such problems can be avoided by asking, "Is it logical for this person to know the information I am looking for?"

If there is any doubt, qualifying questions should be used. Most people are familiar with qualifying questions. They are encountered in surveys that ask how long a person has been a resident of a locale. If a person has been in a locale for less than a year, the next instruction may be to send in the survey without completing any other questions. The short-term resident did not qualify.

It is less common for qualifying questions to be used in interviews. This is due in part to careful selection of interviewees. Where there is some doubt, even after careful selection, qualifying questions should be used. Using the warehouse example, the interviewer might start data collection by asking, "How do you interact with the warehouse?" or "Please comment on how the warehouse relates to your operation." Evaluators will have better data when they qualify their sources.

Another effective way to qualify sources is to ask people who they would recommend talking with about the organization. When a number of people recommend the same source, then confidence in that source grows. An overlooked source is secretaries in an organization. These people are often neglected, but they are rich in information about a company or organization. They are also usually willing to talk with people about what they know.

RECORDING THE EVIDENCE

Not to many people think about how recording evidence is to be done because at face value it seems very simple. However, there is much more to be done than just saving the instruments. When I have been asked to analyze data collected by others, I find they are usually in such disarray that many hours have to be used just to arrange the data in such a way as to make them easy to put into a data base.

A person who builds an instrument should think like a computer, which is extremely linear. A computer counts every item it is going to analyze. Instrumentation should be arranged to do the same thing. Each question should be numbered and each response should also have a number. It is surprising how many instruments do not follow this principle. For example, one instrument had the following questions as items.

>***Please identify from the following list the major source of stress in your personal life during the last 12 months.
>
>1. Consumer prices 2. Death of a family member 3. Raising children 4. High debt load 5. Work overload 6. Unable to sleep at night 7. Close living quarters 8. Illness or health problems.
>
>***Which would you rank as the second most stressful?

No responses for the second question were provided and no instructions about how to "identify" for either question were given to the respondent. Data from these two questions will be mixed at best. The data input person will have a very difficult time recording the information and may even need to make decisions about how to record the data.

The following is another example of a poorly constructed item.

From the following list, identify the three most frequent methods you use to relieve stress.

1. Swear or cuss

2. Drink an alcoholic beverage

3. Get professional help

4. Pray

5. Take a nap

6. Exercise regularly

7. Do something that is relaxing

8. Take some form of medication

9. Change what I am doing and work on something else

10. Sleep on the problem overnight

11. Take a short break and rethink the problem

12. Talk out the problem with another person

13. Other

Each one of these responses could have been scaled with a Likert-type response mechanism rather than asking a person to select the top three. Even with the instruction given, there was no indication if a person should write 1, 2, or 3 in descending order or ascending order. Again, the data will be mixed and the person recording the data will be frustrated. It would have been better if each possible response were its own question with some kind of scale.

With a little patience and forethought, these items could be easily changed to provide easy coding for a secretary or some other person. Recording data means more than merely putting marks on an instrument. Interviewing requires that data be recorded either in written form or electronically stored (audiotapes and videotapes).

ANALYZING THE DATA

Analysis means to break something into smaller parts for examination. When data are analyzed, they are broken into smaller parts so that an examination of the whole can take place. There are various ways to break data into smaller parts. One way is to categorize data. For example, how many people responded that the morale in a company is poor, good, or excellent? Another way to categorize is to break the responses down by respondents units. For example, the evaluator can tally how the people in the warehouse division, the personnel division, the production division, and the sales division responded about an issue. Geography can be another way to analyze data. The way data are broken down is a result of the questions the evaluator is trying to answer. These questions point out how data should be analyzed.

For example, if an evaluator was answering a question concerning how employees of a company feel about management, the question could be answered by categorizing the results; for example, so many feel this way and so many feel that way. However, if the question concerns how employees in the Chicago Office feel about the company as compared to people in the Dallas Office, then the data will be broken into geographical categories.

When qualitative data are analyzed, a matrix approach is useful. After conducting interviews an evaluator will know from the interviews what issues are important. These issues form one side of the matrix, while the group or individuals form the other side. The cells formed by these elements are filled with narrative from the interviews. The whole is now broken into its parts; analysis can go forward. This matrix can be summarized by either reading the columns or the rows. The evaluator can tell how an individual feels about all issues or how all individuals feel about a specific issue. He or she can make marginal summaries that help in forming conclusions. Figure 7.1 shows how these rows and columns form the analysis matrix and how marginal totals or summaries flow from the data cells. The analysis should set the stage for forming conclusions and making recommendations.

FORMING CONCLUSIONS

Conclusions are the judgments and the termination of the study in one sense. After the data are arrayed and the analysis is complete, it is time for the evaluator to make a judgment and say that such and such is the case. If conclusions are not made, then evaluation has not taken place. This is the step that makes data collection, or a study, an evaluation. It is the step that allows the data to be put in a form that will enhance the likelihood that something will happen because of the evaluation.

Many researchers and evaluators are resistant to making

Issues	Individuals Interviewed			
	Person 1	Person 2	Person 3	Issue Summary
Issue A				
Issue B				
Issue C				
Person Summary				

Figure 7.1   Analysis matrix for qualitative data

conclusions. They are used to a safe science that prevents them from moving out from analytical procedures to making statements. Conclusions in evaluation are dangerous and hold implications for the evaluator and for the programs, products, organizations, and people being evaluated. Conclusions need to be justified, and if the steps of choosing indicators, selecting the sources, recording the evidence, and analyzing the data are carefully completed, they will be. If the data line up, the conclusions can be made. For example, if a morale survey is used to gain a baseline in January, and the same valid and reliable instrument is administered in December, then it could be concluded that morale either increased, decreased, or remained the same from one reading to the next.

MAKING RECOMMENDATIONS

Recommendations flow from the conclusions; it is a logical progression. For example, if there are problems in the organization with morale, then it is up to the evaluator to make recommendations about the problem. These recommendations should be more than "the organization should strive to improve morale." Many organizations probably already do this. What is important is that the recommendations be rather specific. For example, "management should use first-line supervisors to introduce new procedures" or "management should be more open with employees by making policy announcements within the company before doing so publicly" are both specific.

Some evaluators may wish to move away from this step by saying, "That's management's job, I only evaluate. Managers are the ones who make decisions and carry them out. I only point out the problems." The counter to such arguments is twofold. First, making recommendations is as much a part of evaluation as is gathering the data, analyzing it, and then forming conclusions. Second, who is more qualified in the organization than the evaluator for making the recommendations? The evaluator knows more than can possibly be reported. The evaluator has a perspective on the problem that management can never achieve without the same hard work and effort the evaluator expends. The evaluator is submerged in data and the context. This is another difference between research and evaluation. Evaluation is aimed at changing problems as a final outcome. It has a practical application in mind when the activities begin.

SUMMARY

Indicators were discussed in terms of how they should be selected in contrast to what should be selected. Important to this discussion is the idea that all evaluations are political. A system for determining how vague indicators can be made specific was explored. Setting standards was discussed in terms of minimally acceptable levels, maximum levels, and the costs of collecting data at various levels. A matrix for analyzing qualitative data was presented and discussed. Forming conclusions and making recommendations were discussed in terms of a close alliance between evaluation and organization development.

CHAPTER 8

Concluding Thoughts

Evaluation is an art form. It is not a science. We may use scientifical tools; however, they are seldom applied with the control that science hopes to achieve. Replication with similar results is an important tool of science. In evaluation, the problem is that things change from moment to moment and a laboratory situation can never be attained. Nor would an evaluator want to. Evaluators want things to change because of evaluation. They may try to emulate science as much as possible, but the fact remains that science cannot be faithfully adhered to. That kind of a situation may make some feel sad, but to others it is a cause to rejoice. Freedom to examine programs, people, organizations, services, and products in ways that are sensible, rigorous, and logical provide the field of evaluation with challenges and opportunities.

Another difference between evaluation and science is evaluation's ethic of valuing. Science offers only description, control, prediction, and explanation. Evaluation offers worth, merit, value, judgment, and change. If an evaluator has these adjectives in mind, he or she will be operating at appropriate levels for evaluation and beyond science.

The other thought has to do with helpfulness. Because it does not deal in values, science cannot be concerned with future states of programs, organizations, people, and the like. Critical theory as a reaction to science offers the notion of changing situations that are oppressive. Evaluators may find some sense of purpose in critical theory.

A recent example can be given here. We were hired to evaluate a large social service program. We found there was a lack of trust at every level of the program. We could have, as scientists, measured the affects of this lack and reported its effects. As dutiful scientists, our work would be done. But as I have said elsewhere in this book, I believe evaluation transcends science into the area of helping people. We gathered together the various people involved in the program, reported our findings, and then asked them what they were going to do about it. We wanted to change the situation.

This example employs the notion of praxis or reflective action. Praxis means thinking about our actions. If one has action without reflection, then one has mindless reaction. If all one has is reflection, then one has merely dreams. Combining the two provides intelligent action.

Evaluation should be helpful; if not, sponsors of evaluation have expended resources in a futile project. Whose responsibility is it to make sure evaluation is a helpful activity? Because evaluators are looked to for direction in the evaluation design, data collection, interpretation, and recommendations, the responsibility falls squarely on the evaluator's shoulders.

Evaluation is an ever-changing enterprise. No two evaluations are the same. Even when an evaluation is repeated, some things have changed such as time, people involved (different people and people who have changed within themselves), and the context of the evaluation. There is much to be learned about evaluation. Hopefully this book has sensitized the reader to some of those things.

EVALUATING OUTCOMES

Outcomes can be thought of as human, programmatic, or organizational impacts. Impacts are among the highest levels of Bennett's hierarchy as discussed in chapter 2. If results are evaluated, then these efforts can be considered "impact evaluation."

Most training managers and adult educators seem to think that waiting until a program or a reorganization has reached a conclusion is the appropriate time to evaluate. In reality, the time to begin thinking and planning and doing an evaluation is when a program or organizational change is being thought about, planned, and executed.

THINKING ABOUT AN EVALUATION

When a program idea is generated or when potential organizational change is considered, an evaluator should be thinking, "How will I know if this program has had any effect on learners, or if the change has had any effect on employees or clients?"

There are many ways a program or change can affect individuals. It can cause them to feel differently about themselves, it can cause them to behave differently, it can cause them to think differently. In terms of evaluation, the problem is how I will be able to demonstrate that these kinds of effects have taken place. If someone feels differently about themselves, then the evaluator could ask them about changes in feelings and have that count as evidence.

Recently, I did an evaluation for an experimental day care program. One of the planned outcomes was an increase in self-esteem in the youngsters attending the program. As the program directors and I met, I asked them what they would accept as evidence that self-esteem had increased. We agreed that parents' statements about self-esteem would be acceptable. Once acceptable evidence was selected, then many other questions were answered such as "What are the sources of evidence?" and "How can I get that evidence?" It seems clear that in this example we had to get the evidence from parents and that the best way would be to interview them. Some hard core number crunchers will not accept this notion of evidence gathering. Remember, evaluation is building a strong case of the best evidence for outcomes; it is not "proving" that a program caused the change.

PLANNING OUTCOME EVALUATION

In the discussion of planning an evaluation, doing an evaluation in terms of data collection has also been considered. However, other important parts of evaluation are seldom completed. One of those is reporting or sharing the results with stakeholders. This aspect is often neglected or is done poorly once data are collected. This may be due to not planning to report, or not liking to write, or not knowing how to present evaluation results.

Just like evaluating, there are several steps or considerations in building a report. One of those is to think about the purpose of the report. Is it to make a pronouncement about a program or is it to help the program develop further? Maybe it is a combination of both (this is quite common). Understanding what is expected from the report will go a long way in helping construct the report.

Another consideration is the audience for the report. Is it an immediate boss? Is it his or her boss? Is it instructors or participants in a program? Is it the funder of the program? Answers to these questions will help an evaluator better organize the material to be presented. It also helps if the evaluator knows how his or her audience(s) prefers to receive information. A verbal report with handouts may be better than a written report. One general rule of thumb to follow is that the shorter the report, the better.

As mentioned in an earlier chapter, I like to divide my reports into three sections, each one a little longer than the preceding section. The first is usually a one-page summary of the findings in point form. These conclusions can stand independently from the rest of the report. (Indeed, each section could stand independently from the others.) The second section is narrative in style, explains the methodology and conclusions, and gives some summary data in tables and graphs. The third section is often massive amounts of data for each question asked. I have used computer printouts from the Statistical Package for the Social Sciences (SPSS) program or transcripts of interviews (with careful attention to preserve the anonymity of the interviewees where necessary) as the content of this section. These three sections allow people with different levels of understanding about evaluation to make judgments about what has been done.

All adult educators or trainers do not necessarily need to follow this format. However, they do need to think about why they construct their reports the way they do. Certainly the goal or objective of the report itself will drive the way the report is constructed. Whether the report is oral, written, or video will depend on the audience, the purpose, and the budget for the evaluation.

One final word about evaluation reports: At some time in his or her activities, an evaluator may need to deal with the press. Not many evaluations deal with controversial issues, but one or two might. Some people suggest that reporters be trained in what certain terms mean so they can better understand evaluation reports. Because reporters and evaluators are both extremely busy, this is not very practical. Another suggestion some have made is for an evaluator to prepare a press release. One problem with this is that the data collected does not belong just to the evaluator. It also belongs to the other stakeholders involved. Another suggestion for evaluators that always applies is to be honest with the press.

Once our evaluation team was giving an oral report to a school district committee about a controversial district policy. We had determined that because it was a preliminary report, we did not want to hand out anything in writing. We did not invite the press, nor did the school district, but the press showed up.

I had alerted the presenters to be aware that the press might well come because of the nature of the controversy and to be ready. (We had proponents as well as opponents on our advisory committee, and one of them may have alerted the press. We still don't know how they knew about the meeting.) One member of the press tape recorded the report and another was furiously taking notes. I feared they would report things that were inaccurate. We followed the suggestion above and were honest with the press. I leaned over to the assistant superintendent who had contracted for the evaluation and said,

"Let's give them all of the numbers we have to make certain they get it right." He quickly agreed. One of my colleagues went a step further and offered to give an interview to the newspaper and to the radio station reporter.

Honesty is not limited to the press. While evaluators have to exhibit a high degree of interpersonal skills as they deal with all of the stakeholder groups involved in evaluations, they must also be honest with them. Sometimes the news is hard to hear, but it must be heard to be helpful. Honesty and helpfulness will serve evaluators well.

Evaluation is an exciting and useful activity. I have seen evaluation teams share frustration and joy as they deal with people and organizations. It can become frustrating when hard news must be reported, but hard news is that which is of most benefit to organizations and people. A friend of mine is well known for the phase "learning occurs at the margin." By that he means that learning occurs more often from failures and difficult situations than it does when everything is going smoothly. Evaluation often points to and explores the margin. It is a brave organization that is willing to look at itself. While evaluators are not necessarily looking for bad or good, they often concentrate on problems that need to be corrected. This kind of activity does take a strong person or organization. It also takes a strong evaluator to deliver the news.

APPENDIX

Personnel Evaluation Matrix
for an Adult Educator

This graph displays work categories and rating categories for an adult educator. Each cell contains a specific description of activities for a given work category at a given level of performance. Reading the cells vertically describes a person's job performance at any given level. Reading the cells horizontally presents a range of performance for any given work category.

Work categories	Unacceptable	Below Expectation	Meets Expectation	Exceeds Expectation	Extraordinary
Service (to the community, profession, county, state, university, national and international)	No involvement with community, state, university, county, or profession.	Holds membership or ad hoc assignments. Not active in organizations or in assignments.	Active member and provides leadership at local level. Active in subcommittees.	Provides leadership at local level and is actively involved at state or national level.	Provides leadership at local, state, and national levels.
Group teaching	Does not teach in a group.	Teaches in a group setting less than 5 times a year and scores 1 standard deviation below the state mean on the teacher evaluation instrument.	Teaches in group setting at least 5 times a year and scores within 1 standard deviation from the state mean on the teacher evaluation instrument.	Teaches more than 5 times a year and scores above 1 standard deviation from the state mean on the teacher evaluation instrument.	Teaches at least 7 times a year and scores above 2 standard deviations from the state mean on the teacher evaluation instrument.
Publishes educational materials	Produces no original educational materials.	Produces non-original educational materials. (Only reproduces materials developed by others.)	Produces and facilitates production of educational materials on a countywide basis.	Materials are used on an area or statewide basis.	Materials are used in refereed regional or national forums.
Evaluate and document impacts	No attempt made to evaluate	Informally evaluates or does so in an unplanned (no preplanning) manner. Bases impacts on assumptions, uses only instructor evaluation form.	Conducts at least one formal, reliable, and valid evaluation in a program area and writes a report.	Designs and implements evaluations that are valid and reliable. Results are used.	Agent develops implications based on valid and reliable evaluations beyond county. These are used by others.

Work categories	Unacceptable	Below Expectation	Meets Expectation	Exceeds Expectation	Extraordinary
Teaching methods	Unwilling to try new methods.	Does not demonstrate willingness to learn and test new teaching methods.	Learns and tests new and innovative teaching methods.	Innovative methods are successfully used and documented.	Teaches others who adopt new methods, or others adopt their own.
Assesses needs	Does not perform needs assessment. Ignores informal input.	Solicits input from few groups or individuals. Advisory council is ineffective.	Gathers input from advisory council and involves them in setting priorities. Uses appropriate stakeholders in the process.	Uses functional advisory committee that represents county clientele. Formal needs assessment is conducted that meets standards of validity and reliability.	Global trends are considered in needs assessment. Results of formal needs assessments are published widely; results are shared and used widely.
Use of instructional material	Fails to provide available instructional materials to clients.	Aware of but does not use appropriate instructional materials.	Maintains or knows how to access instructional materials. Uses instructional materials.	Aware of learning styles and uses a variety of instructional material to accommodate learning differences.	Analyzes learning styles and provides appropriate instructional materials and evaluates impacts.
Facilitation	Refuses to schedule, promote, and organize accessible expertise to address identified problems based on needs assessment.		Makes and produces educational opportunities based on needs. Schedules, promotes, and organizes learning opportunities.		

Work categories	Unacceptable	Below Expectation	Meets Expectation	Exceeds Expectation	Extraordinary
Teamwork (applies to all areas of activity)	Works only alone. Does not share information or accept assistance from others.	Relies on team, but does not contribute to its success or efforts.	Actively seeks opportunities for team efforts. Shares information willingly.	Is a team leader. Initiates or provides formal and informal leadership. Seeks input, maintains group, helps define tasks.	Provides mentoring efforts for other team members.
Continuing education/ professional development	Fails to enroll or attend in-service training programs.	Does not have a plan, but does enroll and attend in-service training programs.	Has a plans for in-service training, enrolls, attends, and applies results of training.	Obtains continuing education beyond company sponsored training. Reads professional literature and applies learnings.	Engages in self-initiated learning and shares outcomes with peers which has positive result for clients.
One-on-one instruction	Gives out misinformation that causes damage.	Only provides iinformation as requested. (Does not provide learning on an interactive basis.)	Agent has a plan to contact targeted audiences as defined by needs assessments. Assists clients in decision making.	Provides documented evidence in contacting target audiences and positively impacts their situations.	Actively seeks and discovers "windows of opportunities" for one-on-one teaching and replicates in other areas. Impacts are positive.
Image	Detracts from organization's image either vocally or in written format.	Has little or no effort at projecting organization's image. Has no understanding of organizational image.	All written materials have an organization identifier (logo). Represents self as an organization member.	Writes and uses press releases about county-based programs. Is sought after by press and other media when news items regarding organization are presented.	Press releases written are used on a district and state-wide basis. Teaches other faculty members in public relations skills and programs.

Work categories	Unacceptable	Below Expectation	Meets Expectation	Exceeds Expectation	Extraordinary
Organizes groups	Has no meetings with groups, clubs, or special interest groups. Ignores groups that are already established. Ignores requests for help in organizing groups.	Makes no effort to organize groups. Maintains non-productive groups, councils, etc.	Assists in organizing councils, clubs, special interest groups relating to program development and implementation.	Seeks out new areas where groups are subsequently organized for support of new programmatic thrusts.	Provides initial leadership in organizing new groups for support of new program thrusts.
Reports	Does not report or rarely provides reports.	Reports are irregular in frequency and quality. Reports are consistently late.	Reports program progress and accomplishments to university and Extension administration, county officials, and local citizens.	Reports are used by the above groups in reporting to the state and federal levels.	Reports are used by the Federal Partner in reporting to Congress and the nation.
Office management	Refuses to budget, write reports, and coordinate with others.	Sporadically budgets, reports, and coordinates.	Budgets, reports, coordinates, and manages office.	Involves others in and out of the office in establishing budgets, writing reports, and coordinating endeavors. Seeks other sources of extension funding.	Secures outside sources of funding to support organizational programming. Does multi-agency reports. Is looked to for Extension's involvement by other local groups.

REFERENCES

Bennett, C. F. (1976). *Analyzing impacts of extension programs*. (Extension Circular 5-575). Washington, DC: Science and Education Administration, United States Department of Agriculture.

Brinkerhoff, R. O. (1987). *Achieving results from training*. San Francisco: Jossey-Bass.

Eisner, E. W. (1975). *The perceptive eye: Toward the information of educational evaluation*. Invited address at the American Education Research Association, Washington DC.

Elman, S. E., & Smock, S. M. (1985). *Professional service and faculty rewards; Toward an integrated structure*. Washington, DC: National Association of State Universities and Land Grant Colleges.

Frankel, J. R., & Wallen, N. E. (1990). *How to design and evaluate research in education*. New York: McGraw-Hill.

Gay, L. R. (1991). *Educational research: Competencies for analysis and application*. New York: Macmillan.

Guba, E. G., & Lincoln, Y. S. (1981). *Effective evaluation*. San Francisco: Jossey-Bass.

Guba, E. G., & Lincoln, Y. S. (1989). *Fourth generation evaluation*. Newbury Park, CA: Sage.

Infobases International Inc. (1992). *Famous quotes* [Computer database]. Orem, UT.

Knowles, M. S. (1980). *The modern practice of adult education*. Chicago: Association Press.

Leedy, P. L. (1989). *Practical research: Planning and design*. New York: MacMillan.

Mager, R. F. (1970). *Analyzing performance problems*. Belmont, CA: Fearon-Pitman.

Mager, R. F. (1972). *Goal analysis*. Belmont, CA: Lear Siegler, Inc./Fearon.

Muller, M. (1991). Quality means results. *Journal of Extension*, 29, 10–14.

Patton, M. (1982). *Practical evaluation*. Beverly Hills, CA: Sage.

Scriven, M. (1981). Product evaluation. In N. L. Smith (Ed), *New techniques for evaluation*. (pp. 121–166). Beverly Hills, CA: Sage.

Smith, M. F. (1991). Criteria for judging excellence. *Journal of Extension*, 29, 14–16.

Smith, M. F. (1989). *Evaluability assessment: A practical approach*. Norwell, MA: Kluwer Academic.

Stufflebeum, D. L. (1983). The CIPP model for program evaluation. In G. F. Madaus, M. Scriven, & D. L. Stufflebeum (Eds.), *Evaluation models: View points on educational and human services evaluation*. (pp. 117–141). Boston, MA: Kluwer-Nijhoff.

Wiktin, B. R. (1984). *Assessing needs in educational and social programs*. San Francisco: Jossey-Bass.

Worthen, B. R., & Sanders, J. R. (1987). *Educational evaluation: Alternative approaches and practical guidelines*. New York: Longman.

INDEX